RIBBLE

Roger Davies

Contents

Front cover:
A Saturday afternoon in Wigan in the early 1970s, featuring PD2/Burlingham 1431, a Leopard/Plaxton and a Lowlander, as well as the backs of a lowbridge Atlantean and a PD3. Also present are a Wigan Corporation Atlantean/Northern Counties and a Lancashire United Plaxton something or other, while visible on the left is Ribble's booking office at 21 Hope Street. Glory Days indeed! *David A. Powell*

Back cover:
What a late-1960s Ribble coach looked like. But hang on . . . 943 was a Scout motor, ending up with Standerwick; what's all this about? Well, it was the 1968 Director's visit, and this coach, only months old, was repainted, re-seated (note the armchairs) and re-heated for the occasion. *David A. Powell*

Title page:
An all-time classic Ribble type was the Leyland Atlantean. The Company's final order for the original PDR1/1 version was for 14, in 1962, all of which had remarkably long lives, lasting until 1981/2. No 1811 is seen here in classic Lancashire surroundings at Haslingden. *Dave Cousins*

First published 2005

ISBN 0 7110 3038 3

Published by Ian Allan Publishing

an imprint of Ian Allan Publishing Ltd, Hersham, Surrey KT12 4RG.
Printed in England by Ian Allan Printing Ltd, Hersham, Surrey KT12 4RG.

Code: 0503/B1

Introduction

I'm writing about something that doesn't exist anymore. Not just Ribble Motor Services, a huge territorial bus company sitting astride North West England, a household name and way of life to countless people. No, not just Ribble that survived Nationalisation, political panicking that it was too big despite numerous municipal and PTE-owned bus fleets in its area, and finally succumbed to the relentless march of late-20th-century UK corporatism, but them all. Listen, you can still catch their memories. This is all their stories, told in human scale, not definitive history, using one of the greatest of them all, Ribble. The Company is still remembered with huge fondness — all the myriad of contacts made with me spoke highly of it. As one person said, 'Ah, Ribble — *there's* a bus company that can be in the same sentence as "Glory".' So, it's for you all, the many, many who relied on, in one way or other, who were, put simply, touched by 'The Ribble'. And for others, who can see through these pages fond memories and associations with other greats in their Glory Days, sit back, relax, enjoy.

How to use this book

This is a big story and a small book. It attempts to give the flavour of Ribble, what it was like to be part of it. As such, it tries to draw out the personal side, the wonderful 'Ribble Family' still very much alive today. The story is there, and one of the great things about this series is that the Author pretty much chooses when the Glory Days were. It seems to me it was the 1950s and, particularly, the 1960s, when Ribble appeared mighty. I say 'appeared', and, well, read on. You may be disappointed that your area, bus type or route gets scant mention, but there was a lot of it, and I've chosen to give specific examples rather than try to do justice to every aspect. I have had to make painful decisions, to concentrate largely on Ribble itself; for example, very few of the buses it took over appear here. There remains much to tell.

A word about red. Ribble buses were a distinctive shade of red known (hardly surprisingly) as 'Ribble Red'. It is notoriously difficult to capture on film. I have chosen to use colour pictures where the red is just about perfect. If in doubt I had many excellent black-and-whites to select from. A few shots were of such exceptional interest that I compromised; I feel sure you will agree it was worth it. Also, some pictures were untraceable, so my thanks to those who took them; I hope you will appreciate their inclusion, and my apologies for the lack of credit. Finally, my sincere thanks to all who contacted me with their Ribble memories, any mistakes, however, are all mine.

Roger Davies
Linton, Kent
November 2004

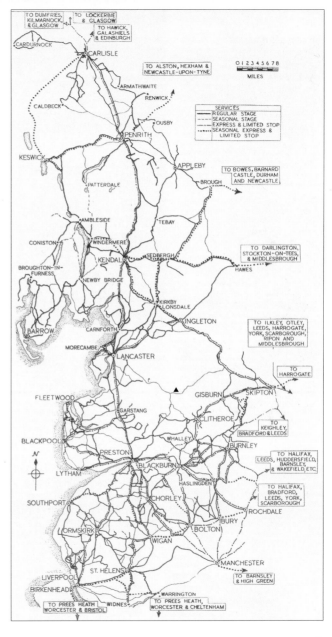

There are some fabulous buses, and then there are these magnificent machines. Thankfully the ex-Tilling gusto of NBC's engineering supremos was somewhat curbed, and this style of Park Royal-bodied AN68 was allowed, Ribble building up a healthy fleet of 104 (none of which is believed to survive). Entering Ribble service at the same time as the author, many worked on Merseyside, and 1315 is here turning just before St George's Hall in central Liverpool. Just look at the window cleaner behind the bus!
David A. Powell

A bus front fleetname plate.
Roger Davies collection

Front Ender

Frenchwood Avenue, Preston, sounds like a splendid tree-lined boulevard but is, in fact, a fairly normal terraced suburban thoroughfare of the type commonplace in North West England. Perched commandingly on a prime corner site — the highest point in town — was the Head Office of Ribble Motor Services. In September 1975, I ascended the imposing staircase to the entrance for my first day with the Company. I was on a three-week induction course, two of which were to be spent here, an emporium always referred to as 'Frenchwood'. My first contacts were a couple of senior traffic officers who got straight down to important business. 'Are you taking lunch?' It seemed a good idea. 'Fine, sign here, you're in "B" Mess.' There were four Messes, 'A' to 'D'. 'D' was for staff from the attached Central Works and conjured up the vision of fitters astride oil-drums

delving into Tupperware boxes of sandwiches. 'B' and 'C' shared the same cuisine, 'C' (for the lower ranks) being self-service, 'B' enjoying waitress service. 'A' wove ideas of potted palms and wicker chairs, where the odd dry sherry and produce of Havana could be savoured in senior company. Indeed, the allocation of a silver napkin-ring therein meant you had arrived. With some trepidation I sat at the end of a longish table of complete strangers. The waitress considered me carefully and, in a tone symptomatic of 1970s catering enquired: 'Who are you and where are you from?' Clearly Assistant Area Superintendent (Northern) was of sufficient stature, and luncheon was served. I had arrived at the mighty Ribble.

Part One: The Rise of Ribble

1. Great Oaks and All That

Gregson Lane, in Lancashire, isn't a lane at all. It's a village. It was once a lane, being part of Higher Walton on the Preston–Blackburn road. It grew on the back of its cotton mills and dyeing works, coming about as a result of its position near the many brooks flowing into the River Darwen. A local resident, James Hodson, started a carting business in the early 1900s, using his vehicles to carry cotton during the day and as buses at night to take the workers home. At the same time, at the other end of the country, Maidstone & District was doing the opposite, replacing bus bodies with lorry ones to carry Kent produce to London overnight. In 1910 Mr Hodson decided to start a regular bus service to Preston, which he carried on himself until 1919. Two timber barns were used as garages, an adjoining stone building serving as a workshop and office. It was this early, tiny venture that eventually became the huge Ribble Motor Services.

Following the Great War many bus services started up using ex-military vehicles and people who had been trained as drivers by the Army. The war brought the fledgling company one major benefit. And it was major in more than one way, being in the form of one Major Harold Edward Hickmott, late of the Royal Flying Corps. His home was Rotherham, and during the Great War he had served with Vickers Armstrong in Barrow-in-Furness. He was gallant and brave, no doubt, but of greater interest to our tale is the fact that, prewar, he had been an Area Manager with a certain bus company — Southdown of Brighton. Throughout their history, there always was a kind of North/South, red/green link between that company and Ribble, even to their choice of unusual full-fronted double-decker buses in the 1950s and '60s.

How interesting that we can trace it this far back. By happy chance, Major Hickmott lighted upon Preston, and, no doubt having fond memories of prewar days, teamed up with Mr Hodson.

On 15 May 1919 trading began on a larger scale, using five buses covering 13 route miles, pending incorporation of a company to take over from Mr Hodson's. This was to be called 'Ribble', after the local river. It's an interesting piece of early marketing: if one looks at the company history and geography, 'Darwen' would have been more appropriate at that time, but the new owners clearly realised Preston was by far the better business prospect. The incorporation took place on 6 June 1919, and shortly afterwards the first private hire was undertaken, charged at £8. The Ribble story had begun.

2. Ten Stirring Years

An oft-used study (but one too important to be left out) is this example of the buses taken over from Hodson. CK 471 was a Karrier — a popular type of the day, built just over the Pennines, in Huddersfield. Fitted with a 36-seater body, it was bought by Hodson in November 1918, having been new in 1913. It is seen outside the Harris Museum & Art Gallery in Market Square, Preston, in company with driver Chris Sutton and conductor Sam Nutter. We can surely forgive Elsie Taylor her hiding tactics; despite having no sense of direction whatever, this 23-year-old did all the worksheets, timetables and rosters and was often to be seen going around the routes, checking mileages. Given the primitive nature of the vehicles such as CK 471, drivers would often let her sit up next to the engine to keep warm.
Mike Shires Ribble collection

Major Hickmott served the Company for 26 hectic years, being its spokesman and responsible for much of its development into a force to be reckoned with in the bus business. Here's an example. The British Automobile Traction Co, a subsidiary of the powerful British Electric Traction, had, in December 1919, started to run four buses in Preston. To the fledgling Ribble this must have looked decidedly dodgy, but the Major was not to be deterred. Minute 37 of the Board meeting of 26 January 1920 notes that the Major had been in touch with the directors of BAT to safeguard Ribble's interests and was meeting them in Preston that very afternoon. He was given full power 'to deal with the directors of BAT as he thought best'. The outcome, on 1 April, was the sale of BAT's four buses to Ribble and the acquisition by BAT of some Ribble shares, allowing the nominal capital of the company to rise from £20,000 to £40,000 to help in its development. Thus started an association with BET that was to last until 1968, by which time the capital invested in the business would be over £6,800,000.

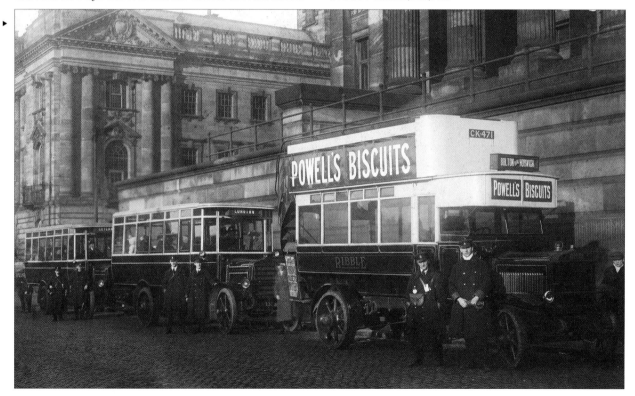

Interesting that. As with many things, it rather depends on where you were sitting at the time. Ribble folklore has it as a splendid victory over BAT, but one Elsie Taylor, taken over with BAT, saw it quite differently. She thought BAT won, and, when you look back at the jewel in the crown that Ribble became, she may have had a point. But we are talking about a new, young, rapidly growing industry here; who could have known how things would turn out? As an example, Elsie lived in Lancaster and had to travel to Preston by train. There simply wasn't a bus; Ribble hadn't done it yet. So BET got Ribble and the Major's entrepreneurial skills, he got their money to expand. Seems like they both won. It is interesting to note that the 1944 Silver Jubilee brochure refers to the whole matter as 'Ribble and BAT were merged into Ribble'.

At first, the central secretarial and administration functions of the Company were undertaken part time by one Harry Cumming, who was an employee of James Todd, chartered accountants of Preston who had worked on the formation of the Company. On a more immediate level, Elsie Taylor had arrived at BAT on 27 December 1919, being based in an office above a cold store supplying grocery shops such as Home & Colonial and Liptons. Major Hickmott made this his base and her his Secretary from April 1920. Elsie was provided with a chair and desk but had to go out and hire a typewriter and cadge an orange box from downstairs to use as a filing cabinet.

A significant happening in 1921 was the opening of the Company's first purpose-built bus garage, in Park Road, Preston, housing 30 buses and remaining in use until 1952. It was the start of a major policy of property ownership.

Ribble became a public company from 1923 and its capital was increased to £100,000 from the following year. By then, such was the growth in the business, that a full time Company Secretary was required. Mr R. T. Ebury was the successful applicant, and he went on in 1933 to be the General Manager of East Yorkshire of Hull and later Western Welsh of Cardiff. He certainly made his mark on the bus industry but is best remembered at Ribble for being a legendary sportsman, donating the Ebury shield to the Central Sports Committee for the snooker league. Major Hickmott was no mean sportsman himself, being renowned for his prowess on the tennis court. As early as March 1924 he drew the Board's attention to the staff's efforts to establish a sports club; this was in existence by June of that year and had received a donation of £50 from the company — an early and clear example of how it sought to build a family atmosphere.

In 1921 CK 471 came to grief in a fire, and when this was reported to the Major he apparently ran out of the office to check that no one was hurt, only just being stopped in time to be told that the incident had occurred at Wingates, near Bolton! On 9 September it was reported that the matter was being dealt with by the BET Insurance Committee, the Board being advised on 26 October that it had been settled for £541.
Roger Davies collection

It's hard to imagine what those first 10 years up to 1929 were like. The Major had an aggressive and enterprising approach to building a successful business in a rapidly developing industry. He set his sights high, jealously guarded Ribble's interests and was fair but firm with competitors. Many of these sprang up, and they had to be watched, contained and, if for the benefit of the Company, absorbed. The Major's quick and alert mind found the best bargain in the majority of cases.

Contemporary reports describe competition at this time as 'lively' — a typical understatement! Prior to the 1930 Road Traffic Act it was the custom for buses to wait at terminal points for a full load before moving off. It took courage and persistence to adhere strictly to a timetable regardless of the actions of competitors who could get short-term advantage by pirating more popular journeys. But Ribble believed that, if the industry were not to destroy itself, it must be based upon the solid foundation of regularity and reliability, and that is precisely what it did under

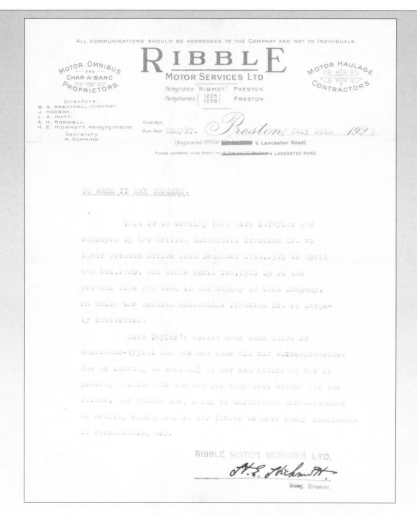

ALL COMMUNICATIONS SHOULD BE ADDRESSED TO THE COMPANY AND NOT TO INDIVIDUALS.

MOTOR.OMNIBUS
AND
CHAR-A-BANC
PROPRIETORS.

RIBBLE
MOTOR SERVICES LTD

MOTOR HAULAGE
CONTRACTORS

Telegrams "RIBMOT", PRESTON.
Telephones { 1225 / 1226 } PRESTON.

Directors:
W. S. WREATHALL, Chairman.
J. HODSON.
L. A. HUNT.
A. H. RODWELL.
H. E. HICKMOTT, Managing Director.

Secretary:
H. CUMMING.

Your Ref.
Our Ref. HEH/ET.

Preston, July 20th 1923

(Registered Office 4 Lancaster Road).

PLEASE ADDRESS YOUR REPLY TO 4 LANCASTER ROAD.

TO WHOM IT MAY CONCERN.

This is to certify that Miss E. Taylor was employed by the British Automobile Traction Co. at their Preston office from December 27th, 1919 to April the 1st, 1920, and since April 1st, 1920 up to the present time has been in the employ of this Company, in which the British Automobile Traction Co. is largely interested.

Miss Taylor's duties have been those of shorthand-typist and she has done all our correspondence. She is leaving us entirely of her own Accord as she is getting married and she has our very best wishes for the future, and should she, owing to unforeseen circumstances, be seeking employment in the future we have every confidence in recommending her.

RIBBLE MOTOR SERVICES, LTD.

H. E. Hickmott

Mang. Director.

Elsie Taylor would just have seen the first Leylands, for on 4 August 1923 she left to get married. Here is her reference from the Major, typed by herself. Like many bus companies at that time, Ribble also referred to itself as a haulage contractor; note also that by now the Head Office had moved.
Kathleen Morris (daughter of Elsie Taylor)

the hazardous conditions that prevailed. Passengers needed to rely on a bus at a given time and fare; anything else would have strangled the business before it was properly organised, so the Company plodded on. It learned the valuable and sharp lesson that costs had to be kept down to the lowest level for it to survive and soon implemented measures such as inter-working of routes to get the maximum productivity from buses and crews.

Mind you, the odd tactic was needed. Desmond Hartley, achieving the age of 11, started to travel from home in Morecambe to the Lancaster Royal Grammar School and became aware of the local buses — red Ribble, blue County and green Morecambe Corporation. He had the choice of blue or red but can only remember travelling by Ribble and sharing the 8.20am and 4.25pm return with girls from their Grammar. The fare was 4d (2p) single, never bought owing to the 6d (3p) return and 2/6d (12p) weekly tickets. And here's the rub: Ribble had lowered its fares, so County was more expensive and disappeared. Desmond's mother said: 'I told you what would happen when Ribble reduced their fares.' Actually, Ribble gradually gained a controlling interest in the firm before it ceased trading, on the last day of 1930. What does clearly bear out Ribble's strategy is Desmond's statement: 'Matter of fact, Ribble always looked more confident and prosperous.' How interesting.

It wasn't just newcomers. The Town Police Clauses Acts of 1847 and 1889 gave local authorities the role of licensing vehicles and staff to ply for hire. Whilst they could not fix timetables, they largely did so by attaching undertakings to vehicle licences. Those with their own transport systems often required protective fares from Ribble and sought in many ways to protect their own interests. Appeals by the Company to the Minister of Transport against refusal of licences and petitions to Parliament against powers sought by authorities that would damage Ribble were frequent. There were also the timid and squeamish local authorities which discouraged bus services, egged on by local tradesmen fearful for their business. The railways had to be watched too: they were not keen to see local services expand at their expense, bearing in mind that they were, in effect, the established operators, and were prone to retaliate.

It is astonishing, given all this, that in those 10 years, driven largely by Major Hickmott's vision, the Company grew at all. But grow it did, mileage increasing between 50 and 100% year on year in each one. At the year ended 31 March 1929 Ribble ran 17½ million miles with a fleet of 474 buses. Fleet strength in May 1919 had been just five.

A significant occurrence in 1923 was the Company's first takeover, of J. Mashiter of Preston, trading under the unlikely name of Tra Bon services. Unless you think naming yourself after a river is unlikely. Ribble itself considers its first major purchase to have been the Chorley Auto Co — all four buses of it — in 1925. Arguably more significant was the absorption in 1927 of fellow BET company Lancashire & Westmoreland of Lancaster, highlighting the march northwards. By the end of 1929 some 23 deals — amalgamations, joint arrangements or outright purchases — had been struck, and no fewer than 20 properties, stretching from Wigan to Penrith, either purchased or built. At the larger centres staff canteens were provided, supervised by manageresses reporting to a head supervisor in Preston. Already a Company Architect, Cecil Quinn, was in place to make sure the buildings were in good condition and properly maintained. The Frenchwood Empire had dawned with the opening of workshops and the first administrative offices in 1926. It is an amazing achievement, and gives a clear indication of the business acumen of the Major and his team.

From these times emerged two significant developments, each of which would be a feature of Ribble for many years. One was the initiation of medium-distance limited-stop express services; the other was co-ordination or joint operation with a myriad of other companies. The first of the former was with North Western Road Car of Stockport and Lancashire United Traction of Atherton in 1928 between Manchester and Blackpool — something that probably deserves the title 'gold mine', soon justifying a 15-minute frequency at weekends. The first of the latter was a 1929 agreement with Haslingden Corporation. Both can be seen in the light of the many other companies that were running buses in Ribble's chosen patch, and both contributed to the vast area the company's buses served.

On 28 December 1929, heralded by Ribble as a 'Momentous Day', the LMS Railway took a substantial shareholding in the Company. Despite very different approaches to public transport (the railway looking to bulk flows, the bus company spreading loads over as long a time as possible), the new arrangements introduced such useful work as reciprocal assistance for breakdowns, inter-availability of return tickets and joint ticketing, including on steamers.

Probably more momentous as far as Ribble staff were concerned was the 1929 appointment, as assistant to the Managing Director, of one Horace Bottomley, of whom we shall hear more in Part Two.

RIBBLE
MOTOR SERVICES LIMITED

PRELIMINARY ANNOUNCEMENT

Issue of 200,000 Six-and a Half Per Cent. Cumulative Preference Shares of £1 Each at Par.

200,000 6½ per cent. Cumulative Preference Shares of £1 each at par will be offered for Public Subscription on Friday, the 21st inst., the Subscription List closing on or before Wednesday, the 26th inst.

Applications from present Shareholders, Company's Employees and residents of the districts served by the Company's Organisation will receive special consideration.

Copies of the Prospectus may be obtained on the 20th inst. from the Company's Enquiry Offices and Agents, the Company's Head Office, Preston, from Brokers, and from any Branch of the Company's Bankers, Westminster Bank Ltd.

Frenchwood Avenue,
PRESTON.
18th September, 1928.

R. T. EBREY,
Secretary.

B. SEED & SONS, PRINTERS, PRESTON.

For : No. 46.

BOROUGH OF LANCASTER.

This is to Certify that *Harry Cartwright*

of *10, Fox St, Preston,*

has been licensed as a Driver of a Motor Omnibus plying for hire within the Borough of Lancaster for the period 1st April, 1929, to 31st March, 1930.

[signature]

Chief Constable.

NOTE.—This Certificate must be carried by the holder at all times when on duty, and must be produced on demand of any passenger carried on the Omnibus, or of any Police Officer.

3. Wot, No Buses?

On 31 May 1921 the Major reported to the Board that an approach had been made by the locally based Leyland company with an offer of reconditioned chassis. The offer was declined. Clearly, Leyland wouldn't take no for an answer, a major decision for both it and Ribble.
Its perseverance paid off, and, following a brief demonstration with another bus, on 16 June 1923 No C62, an SG7 model registered CK 3513, became the first of many Ribble Leylands. Ten more followed that year, and C67 is seen in Preston showing off its two-door, full-front 38-seater body, also by Leyland. Given what had gone before, these buses were revolutionary. The 'C' number referred to the chassis but came to be used as the fleetnumber; there was a separate series of 'B' numbers for bodies. There appear to be pictures on display against the wall; note also the fashions of the time. This bus lasted until 1932, becoming a lorry and serving with Woodhouse of Preston until 1938.
Mike Shires Ribble collection

The June 1919 fleet was made up of buses inherited from Mr Hodson. Perhaps unsurprisingly there is some variation in the reporting of their details, but there is agreement that there were five used in service. The earliest dated from 1913, the most recent from May 1919. There is no doubt that some were Karriers and that this was a favoured make. Indeed, in October 1919 the Company tried unsuccessfully to become an agency for that manufacturer but succeeded with the AEC company from Southall, becoming sole supplier for the area from Lancaster and Morecambe right up to Carlisle. Records only show two sales, so it wasn't exactly a front-line business. Two of the Karriers were double-deckers, the remainder single-deckers. Another double-deck, taken over but not used, was an ABC built by the All British Car Company of Glasgow. A further Karrier was fitted with a flatbed lorry body and used for haulage during the week and fitted with a single-deck coach body at weekends. The Karrier was used for a short time, but, along with the unused double-decker, was soon exchanged for a hand-operated tyre press.

In 1924, after a fleet of 19 full-front SG7s and SGH7s had been built up, the new SG9 model had a half-cab, albeit retaining the two-door arrangement. Maybe Captain Betteridge, in charge of engineering and very influential in terms of vehicle appearance, had some say in the matter. The first SG9, C84, is shown when new and before licensing as CK 3591. It was one of four 38-seaters, subsequent deliveries reducing in capacity to 36 and then 35 before dispensing with the two-door arrangement. This bus lasted until April 1932, again seeing out its time as a lorry (with Teggin of Salford and the Grantham Motor Co), finally bowing out at the end of 1936. *Mike Shires Ribble collection*

As was the case with many other fleets, and certainly those associated with BET, ex-military AEC and Daimler chassis were the basis of Ribble's first buses. These were cheap and rugged, and parts were interchangeable.

The four buses taken over from BAT in April 1920 were all AECs, two having initially been used in Barrow-in-Furness and at least one in Macclesfield, bearing registration letters MA accordingly. Daimler became the favoured choice, being fitted with a quieter engine, but in 1922 some Vulcan buses were bought, fitted with new style 'air pocket' tyres (known as NAP tyres) — precursors to the pneumatic tyres we know today.

By the year ended 31 March 1922 some 29 buses were owned, 648,000 miles had been run and two million passengers had been carried. Ribble did not try again to become an agent for a

Launched at the 1927 Commercial Motor Show, Leyland's Tiger was of a lower build than previous types and introduced the T range of petrol engines that were to last until 1942. Ribble was the first operator to place a large fleet (40) into service, in 1928. No C625 (numbers having leapt ahead as a result of Ribble's buying other bus businesses), a TS2 of 1929, has 26-seat Leyland bodywork with a forward entrance and roof-mounted luggage rack; luggage had previously been carried inside, behind the rear door. Although rather plain, the Tiger was found to be a much better all-weather bus for long-distance services than were contemporary coach designs, which tended to feature canvas roofs. Although sold in 1936, this bus is recorded in use until as late as 1954. *Mike Shires Ribble collection*

At Rigby Road, Blackpool, in June 1931 we find a 1928 Leyland Lion PLSC3, one of the last of the type bought by Ribble, in the care of driver Arthur Marston (left) and conductor Jack Holyland, having just arrived on the express service from Keswick. The coloured postcard suggests the deeper red of the time. Arthur later became Engineering Road Inspector at Carlisle. *Alan Marston (son of Arthur)*

manufacturer; indeed, manufacturers were more interested in the company as a customer. One such was the local Leyland Motors, and on 16 June 1923 No C62, a Leyland SG7 single-deck registered CK 3513, became Ribble's first Leyland. It was the start of a very long and mutually influential relationship.

Leyland's next model, the Lion, achieved 183 sales to Ribble between 1926 and 1928, after which the Company took large numbers of the technically advanced Tiger. In 1929 these were joined by the first of many of the double-deck equivalent, and a bit of a transport icon, the Titan. During this time buses entered the fleet from no fewer than 16 acquired companies. A goodly proportion were Leylands, but examples of Daimler, AEC, Thornycroft and Guy were prominent, with a myriad of one-off purchases. The 1929 fleet of 474 was varied, and no doubt the Major and his team planned a respite and a chance for some standardisation. It was not to be, for one of the greatest upheavals the bus industry has ever faced was about to confront them.

4. 1930 and All That

Things really couldn't go on, and they didn't. The 1930 Road Traffic Act sought to bring order to the industry. It is perhaps a moot point whether order or bureaucracy was its first achievement. Put simply, it required all bus services to be licensed, the whole shooting match being overseen by Traffic Commissioners who would issue these along with licences to companies, buses and crews. It was a task of mind-numbing complexity. The date of the 'Stay Put' order was 9 February 1931, and thereafter each service and every form of activity came under close scrutiny of the Commissioners. Everything had to come to light, from the earliest beginnings, when a road service application, which had attracted representations, was publicly examined. Just as well that, along with everything else, the Major's team had kept records. No fewer than 1,153 applications for services and backings (services travelling through another area) had to be made. Owing to Ribble's extensive long-distance services, some had to be obtained from all areas in the country. A whole new department had to be set up to deal with this ceaseless activity and the almost daily appearance of staff in the Traffic Courts. So much overtime was worked that the father of 14-year-old licensing clerk Tommy Hill became so suspicious that his lad was out every night that he made enquiries to ensure that his son was indeed in work! This overtime was all unpaid but became so commonplace that the Company gave staff involved first one and then another half-week's extra pay.

All this activity meant constant communication with BET, and Ribble was lucky that one of its main points of contact was W. S. Wreathall, who liked short letters and often replied with one-liners!

Ribble was also fortunate in another way. The new legislation strongly emphasised co-ordination between all forms of transport, and Ribble had form in that area. Prior to the Act no fewer than 86 services were either joint or co-ordinated, including such delights as the Liverpool Overhead Railway and Ullswater Transport & Navigation Co. After it a staggering 142 were added, which was so far-reaching that the Company could claim that, with the exception of operators of 'market service' routes in remote areas, it had only three serious competitors on ordinary bus services. It is fair to say that Ribble made the new Commissioners' huge task a lot easier.

In 1929 Ribble bought its first new double-deck bus, an example of the revolutionary Leyland Titan also introduced at the 1927 Show. The first of many of this type (the last being purchased in 1963), C575 was a TD1 model, seating 51 people and costing £1,666 4s; it passed in 1938 to Western SMT and thence to a showman in Glasgow, last being recorded in 1949. *Mike Shires Ribble collection*

5. The Roaring 'Thirties

With bureaucracy, you either knuckle down and get on with it or run away. There can be no doubt that many entrepreneurs, risk-takers or downright opportunists found the 1930 Act all too much. With its Frenchwood powerhouse up and running and becoming a substantial bureaucracy in its own right and the Major's zeal still in full flood, Ribble was well placed to benefit. Up until World War 2 roundly 50 companies came into its fold. There is a whole tale on its own here, but sadly on our brief trip through history we can dwell on only a few notables, interesting in themselves but also indicative of how the Company's area grew.

There must have been a plan. The Mersey seemed a southern border, and sights were set on the Scottish border as a northerly

one. Fellow BET company Lancashire & Westmoreland was absorbed at the end of 1927, bringing a very mixed fleet of 79 buses and, incidentally, a Kendal–Keswick route, the precursor to the famed 555 Lancaster–Keswick route still with us today. The border city of Carlisle was temptingly close, but United from the east, Cumberland from the west and Caledonian from the north seemed more logical to succeed, as they already had toe-holds in this tramway town. But the trams, run by the Balfour Beatty group, were worn-out, and the City Council's application to run its own replacement buses was thrown out by the new Traffic Commissioners. The City Council never forgot, continuing to lay claim on the services even in my time there

In 1930 Ribble took over the Merseyside Touring Co. Here Merseyside staff wave farewell to the green buses in front of the area's largest bus, EM 2422, a Tilling-Stevens petrol-electric six-wheeler with a 64-seat dual-door Massey body quoted as regularly carrying more than 100 people! *Roger Davies collection*

during the mid-1970s! The Commissioners suggested a co-ordination scheme between the major operators and the astonishingly numerous (14) independent operators, and Ribble, somehow, got the job of acting on behalf of the former. The upshot was that Ribble started negotiations with as many of the small companies as it could and bought no fewer than seven of them. By the time the trams ceased, on 21 November 1931, Ribble had come from being a junior player into the largest operator in the city. Carlisle became and remained an important and individual northern outpost of the Ribble empire.

A major purchase in June 1930 (for £120,000), which ultimately established Ribble on Merseyside, was the Merseyside Touring Co, initially retained as a subsidiary, with full takeover following in September 1931. This company, formed only in March 1929, had established a network of services from Liverpool to Bootle, Orrell, Seaforth and Litherland against severe opposition, particularly from Liverpool Corporation. It had itself acquired Nor-West bus services, which had routes in Crosby, Maghull, Ormskirk and Southport and would also be kept as a Ribble subsidiary. In the year prior to Ribble control Merseyside carried 7,500,000 people on its 50 buses, employing 200 staff. An agreement covering Liverpool in 1931 caused Ribble to give up its new

gains to the 'Corpy', which wasn't actually that interested, and rival licence applications led to a newcomer, MacShane's, being granted the routes. This was too much for Ribble, which appealed and got the services back from August 1933, acting as agents for Liverpool Corporation. All this led to much greater trust between the two and, no doubt, the curious situation whereby the Corporation's Litherland depot was further from Liverpool than was Ribble's at Bootle.

In the late 1920s there was a massive surge in interest in long-distance services, no doubt fuelled by the availability of more reliable vehicles offering a real alternative to the train. The route from East Lancashire and Blackpool to London via Birmingham was an obvious draw, and one of the major players (along with three others) was the 1904-established Walter Clinton Standerwick of Blackpool. A further player was Joseph Bracewell, who ran a Colne–London service and one from Blackpool to Birmingham. Standerwick was advertised for sale in 1932 and in November was purchased jointly by Ribble and North Western. Given the Birmingham involvement, the local operator there, Midland Red, was a touch upset, but it seems likely it had supported a rival bid by Bracewell. In any case Ribble bought Bracewell in 1933 and incorporated it with Standerwick. To keep the peace a one-third share of Standerwick was sold to Midland Red, but the whole

Double-deck developments moved on apace, with this type of bus featuring more in Ribble's purchases. Leyland had introduced the oil engine in 1934, and the Company standardised on this for its double-deckers. Bodywork wasn't quite so clear-cut, Ribble being a touch wary about Leyland's new metal-framed design and so sticking with another local builder from Preston, English Electric. To give Leyland a chance, one of its new types was bought in 1935. Whilst 10 more followed in 1936, the remaining 32 double-decks had bodywork from four different bodybuilders, so we can draw our own conclusions. However, Leyland soon introduced a revised metal-framed body and, in 1939, a new Titan — the TD7 — with a number of new features. This was enough for Ribble to order 40, with a further 19 having Brush bodywork. Delivered in 1940, C2338 seen here shows wartime additions such as white edges to the mudguards. There is no doubt that body looks have advanced considerably since 1927.
Mike Shires Ribble collection

arrangement was too cumbersome, and the latter was bought out by Ribble in 1933 with the North Western share following in 1934. Now the sole owner, Ribble elected to keep Standerwick as a separate identity — a far-sighted decision.

Financial pressures at this time must have been continuous. Dealing with the growth of the business, new premises and vehicles and funding developments such as conversion to pneumatic tyres must have been a strain. On top of this, going through the assets of acquired businesses and engaging their staff, on occasion at a level to which they were not suited, must have been demanding. Competitive pressures continued immediately after the 1930 Act, bringing yet more concern.

Costs and revenue were key, so the level of wages and fares was crucial. It seems Major Hickmott kept a close eye on general wage rates and paid slightly over the odds. Apparently conductresses (a more common breed in Scotland) at the Caledonian company were so poorly paid that they tended to move to Ribble as soon as the opportunity arose. Wages were not high in the textile industry, on the Merseyside docks or in the mines around Wigan — all major employers in Ribble's patch. Workers in the famous Carr's biscuit factory in Carlisle could expect about 30s (£1.50) a week, and the city was surrounded by a huge, depressed rural area where the statutory minimum wage was 25s (£1.25) a week. By contrast, Ribble crews could expect over £2 a week for 48 hours' work. But there was a catch: whilst 80-90% of staff worked these hours, others only had 36- or 24-hour guarantees. The 48-hour folk were given five days' holiday, not including a Saturday, those on 36 hours often achieving the same hours but without holidays! Crews on 24-hour guarantees would often wait at depots to pick up any work from staff who failed to turn up. Cashiers earned less, despite handling large sums of cash, the argument being that they were indoors whilst many buses lacked heaters. Jack Brown, who

at under 21 was responsible for the small Church depot near Accrington, earned 25s (£1.25) a week, which made him careful not to lose a single coin! Conductors were issued with only a dustcoat and had to buy their own dark trousers, while office cleaners earned just 4½d (less than 2p) an hour. Nevertheless, Ribble jobs were highly prized. There was a fair amount of turmoil in Carlisle in 1931 when the tramways shut, as not all staff could transfer immediately. One such, Jimmy Smith, was at the cinema one afternoon when someone from Ribble turned up at his house to offer him a job, whereupon a member of his family ran to the cinema and arranged for a message to appear on screen telling him to come home. One seasonal driver at Keswick who hailed from Newcastle spent his nights in a tent, and a cashier at Clitheroe who was not local set up a hammock between filing cabinets and regularly slept overnight at the office! Further improvements in conditions came in 1936 with the introduction of a Pension & Assurance scheme. Among all this a milestone was reached in 1931, when revenue exceeded £1 million for the first time.

Discipline was strict, coming from the Military backgrounds of the Major and Captain Betteridge, who took care of things engineering. It is claimed that if any traffic staff strayed into engineering territory they were sacked. Ron Hopkins recalls that Betteridge toured Central Works at 10.00 every Monday, his Sunbeam company car (one of only two, the Major having a Daimler) being parked and washed by the chauffeur. He was usually accompanied by his terrier dog, which was given attention by staff, often eliciting a brusque 'Get on with your work, laddie!' from the Captain. Behind his back they threw bolts at it. 'Betteridge was not good at industrial relations,' remembers Ron, but one day he met his match in a bodyshop worker named Charlie Evans, who addressed him without using his correct military title. 'When you refer to me in future, laddie, you are to use the title "Captain",' snorted Betteridge. 'And when you refer to me,' replied Charlie, 'you must use my correct title of "Major".'

Things were the same on the Traffic side. An Inspector from the Cumberland company's depot in Millom in the 1930s tells of a day when the Ribble bus outstationed there would not start. Despite being towed around town a few times by a Cumberland vehicle it still would not go, and one trip was lost. The Ribble crew received a day's suspension as a result, something the Cumberland inspector thought a little harsh!

Fares are a tale in themselves. Suffice it to say that prior to 1930 fares evolved very much according to individual circumstances. The new Traffic Commissioners tried to introduce some rationalisation with a standard mileage-based scale, still keeping special workmen's, children's, return and period return fares. Local circumstances still had an influence, and, for example, double the mileage rate could be charged for travel over the Kirkstone Pass. Government action — notably a tax increase on fuel in the 1930s — was justification for raising certain fares, but it has to be said that fare levels remained pretty stable.

A symbolic move on 6 September 1937 was the opening of the splendid new Head Office building, built at a cost of £30,000, across the road from the existing one in Frenchwood. Teddy Dravers well remembers arriving at the old building after a successful interview at BET HQ at 88 Kingsway, Holborn, in front of W. S. Wreathall and Major Hickmott; he describes it as 'a bit of a squeeze', the traffic office being about 40ft square and presided over by one Jezz Swarbrick, who sat in a glass-fronted office overlooking the 'rabble'. Teddy recalls everyone much looking forward to better working conditions and more breathing-space in the new offices. Bruce Maund recalls it increasing staff — a classic case of expanding to fill the space available. There is no doubt that Ribble was hugely centralised and fostered an impressive bureaucracy!

Again, as another decade drew to a close, those at Ribble must have been looking forward to a period of calm. But war clouds were gathering over Europe, and the Company was about to face testing times.

All Ribble double-decks bought new in the 1930s were of the lowbridge style, as shown here. The sunken side gangway and four-abreast seating made them difficult to conduct and no doubt caused a few headaches downstairs. There is at least a heater. This is C1736, a 1937 TD4 with yet another make of bodywork — Brush. In theory 27 people could sit up here, with 26 below. The design wasn't without its benefits, however. Driver Ted Gahan, returning to Aintree depot with postwar 2588 had bought a flowering cherry tree for his new house and had laid it along the sunken side gangway. An inspector boarded and asked Joe, his conductor (or 'guard', in correct Merseyside parlance) if there was anybody upstairs. 'No,' came the reply, 'just a tree.' The inspector laughed but didn't check! *Colin Morris collection*

In 1931 a 19-year-old lad by the name of Nelson was conducting an Appleby–Kirkby Stephen Ribble bus when he met a 16-year-old girl called Dorothy. Love blossomed, and they were married in 1935, Mr Nelson continuing to work for the Company until called up for war service in Burma. On his return he went back to Ribble. During the war Dorothy joined Ribble as a conductress, and this professionally taken picture shows Dorothy in full uniform of navy-blue hat complete with Ribble badge, jacket and skirt with a white shirt and checked tie. Her conductor's licence badge number is CC 19160. She is inserting a ticket from the rack in her other hand into the Willebrew ticket machine. These machines were developed by Williamson's of Ashton-under-Lyne from the invention of Reg Ebury, Ribble Company Secretary, and Edwin Brewer, head of Ticket Audit. Introduced in 1930, they would be phased out by February 1959, last being used at Lancaster and Morecambe.

courtesy Nora Swaby
(daughter of Dorothy Nelson)

◀ Dorothy in a beige overall with navy trim (no doubt summer wear) beside 1938 ECW-bodied Leyland Cheetah 1825. There is a warning triangle for the Dewandre braking system and on the other side a licence plate bearing the number 3597 — a system similar to taxi licences.

courtesy Nora Swaby

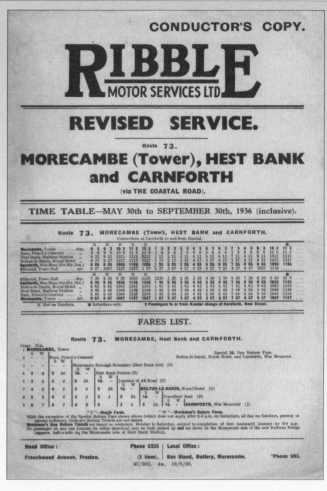

▲ Conductors were issued with time- and fare tables, this being a 1936 example for service 73.
Ribble Enthusiasts' Club

18

The Willebrew system was replaced by the Setright machine, which was also motorised for OMO work. Connie Birchenough, the first conductress at Preston depot to wear trousers, with this machine and the correct perch for the other conducting duty of mountaineering to change the destination blinds. This early-1960s picture also stars 1366, a 1952 all-Leyland PD2/12.
Ribble Enthusiasts' Club

An Ultimate ticket of the type used (in lieu of Setrights) on Carlisle city services from 1949; they were also used on local services in Kendal, Chorley, Fleetwood, Preston and Bootle.
Roger Davies collection

An example of the Setright ticket, introduced first at Wigan on 31 March 1954. *Joe Gornall collection*

RIBBLE MOTOR SERVICES LIMITED
Fleet Allocation. Summer Period
June 24th to September 24th, 1939

Depot	Double Deckers	Cheetahs 32 Str. S.R	30 Str. S.R	30 Str. F.R	Tiger 32 Strs.	Other Saloons	Coaches	Total	Maximum Mid-week Req'mts.
Preston(Park Rd)	10 +17	-	1	2	-	13	4	30	26
Preston(Selborne St)	40 +14	6	-	33	11	1	11	102	84
Blackpool	1 +12	-	-	2	-	6	20	29	21
Fleetwood	+3	-	7	10	-	-	3	20	19
Garstang	3 +1	-	-	2	-	7	-	12	10
Lancaster	2 +8	5	3	6	-	15	5	36	29
Morecambe	12 +3	-	-	1	2	1	13	29	23
Chipping	-	-	-	-	-	1	-	1	1
Knott End	-	-	-	-	-	2	-	2	2
Ingleton	-	-	-	2	-	-	-	2	2
Kirkby Lonsdale	-	-	-	-	-	1	-	1	1
Liverpool	25 -	-	-	-	-	9	12	46	46
Bootle	67 +10	6	-	2	3	29	34	141	100
Ormskirk	2 +5	-	-	-	7	4	-	13	12
Wigan	3 +25	-	-	-	13	24	2	42	32
Chorley	12 +6	5	-	-	7	17	3	44	41
Bolton	3 +3	6	-	19	-	-	-	48	24
Manchester	-	-	-	-	-	-	13	13	13
Widnes	-	-	-	-	-	-	1	1	1
Blackburn(George St.)	14 +12	2	7	3	6	5	18	55	47
(Foundry Hill)	-	4	-	-	7	5	-	16	16
Burnley	6 +4	6	-	17	-	12	33	74	60
Clitheroe	3 +4	-	-	-	-	15	6	24	20
Accrington	-	-	-	-	-	8	12	20	15
Skipton	-	-	-	4	-	5	3	12	11
Rochdale	-	-	-	-	-	1	-	1	1
Kendal	-	-	12	16	-	3	7	38	31
Ulverston	6 +7	-	5	-	-	8	2	21	19
Dalton	2	-	-	-	-	7	-	9	9
Sedbergh	-	-	-	-	-	2	-	2	2
Grange	-	-	2	-	-	-	-	2	2
Millom	-	-	-	-	-	1	-	1	1
Ambleside	-	+1	-	9	3	-	3	15	13
Penrith	-	-	18	3	-	-	6	27	22
Carlisle	24 +6	-	-	-	6	22	6	58	54
Keswick	-	-	3	-	-	-	4	7	7
Shap	-	-	-	-	-	-	1	2	1
Kirkby Stephen	-	-	2	-	-	-	-	2	2
Appleby	-	-	-	-	-	-	1	1	1
Kirkoswald	-	-	-	1	1	-	-	2	2
Bowness	-	-	-	-	-	2	-	2	2
Glasgow	-	-	-	-	-	-	1	1	1
Scarborough	-	-	-	-	-	-	1	1	1
Edinburgh	-	150	-	-	-	-	1	1	1
Middlesbrough	-	8	-	-	-	-	1	1	1
	235 377	40	71	126	63	225	246	1006	

NOTE. Preston and Penrith totals include 8 vehicles and 3 coaches respectively for Engineering purposes on Saturdays. All large seating capacity vehicles to remain as at present allocated.

14/6/39.

The fleet allocation at the outbreak of war. The pencil additions to the double-deck list almost tally with the total of the last TD5s of 1939 (24), the TD7s (69) and the Utilities (58), so may tell us where the additional double-decks went during the war. Mrs Barnes' Penrith one is there! And just look at the allocation of one coach each to Glasgow (BS), Scarborough (no code), Edinburgh (CM) and Middlesbrough (CF)! *Joe Gornall collection*

6. More War

During the war traditional bus suppliers were heavily committed to war production. New bus-building came under Government control, and only a few suppliers were left, providing little choice and a standardised product known as a 'Utility'. Between 1943 and 1945 Ribble received 58 such buses, which, compared with prewar purchasing levels, gives some indication of the pressures under which the Company was working. A mixture of Guys and Daimlers, with five different makes of bodywork, all would be subject to much rebuilding postwar, but this doesn't stop Joe Gornall remembering one in the early '50s as 'an owd Guy wi' wooden seats' used for his trips from Great Eccleston to Elswick to visit relatives on their farm . . . or maybe to Bond's Café, with its famous ice cream. Anyway, notable were eight Park Royal-bodied Guys which were the first centre-gangway (as opposed to the sunken side gangway) highbridge types to be purchased new and were allocated to Carlisle. They clearly led the way to the purchase postwar of this much more user-friendly type of bus. No 2394, seen here in Lancaster, was a Daimler CWG5 with Brush bodywork. *David A. Powell collection*

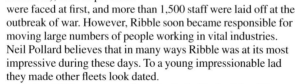

It is difficult to grasp just what it must have been like to live through these times. There are the bare facts, but it is through the eyes of those who were there that we get some semblance of the reality. Ribble started off on a good footing, with a fleet average age of 2¾ years. Throughout the war, despite shortages of skilled staff and materials, high standards were maintained. The fleet remained remarkably stable at around the 1,050 mark and fares were held at 1931 levels. As the largest operator of express services in the country and with many rural services (all of which were an early target of the Regional Transport Commissioner for suspension to conserve resources), serious problems were faced at first, and more than 1,500 staff were laid off at the outbreak of war. However, Ribble soon became responsible for moving large numbers of people working in vital industries. Neil Pollard believes that in many ways Ribble was at its most impressive during these days. To a young impressionable lad they made other fleets look dated.

During 1939 company staff serving in the Territorial and Reserve forces were mobilised, and women taken on as conductors. Military commitments were undertaken — on one occasion a whole battalion was moved without a hitch from Merseyside to Leicestershire — and some buses were requisitioned or kept in reserve as ambulances. As the situation worsened in 1940, provision was made by the Ministry of War Transport for vital emergency services in the event of invasion. Heavy bombing affected Merseyside, causing much grief and destruction, but thankfully no staff members lost their lives while on duty.

Don Kelly started what was to become almost a 45-year career as an 18-year-old conductor at Bootle on August Bank Holiday Monday in 1940. His father had to agree to make up any cash shortages due to his age. When the air-raid siren sounded, bus crew and passengers had to make for a shelter, not emerging until the 'All Clear'. He remembers on many occasions the last bus from Liverpool arriving back at Bootle after the first one of the next morning had left. Many a night he walked home with shrapnel clanging off his tin hat. After VE Day he started a clerical career that ended at Frenchwood. Despite the alarming beginning to his career he says: 'I enjoyed my life at Ribble. I can honestly say I never moaned about the job and never thought of leaving.'

Major Hickmott was so concerned about the situation on Merseyside that he loaded his car with food (where he got it from remains unclear!) and drove down to Liverpool for it to be distributed amongst affected staff. Shortly afterwards he invited the Senior Clerk and his family — and likely others — to have the run of house and grounds at his private residence, 'Hermitage', in Grimsnargh.

Ivy Laycock was in the WAAF. Returning home on leave, in uniform, she arrived at Carlisle by train to continue her journey to Kendal by Ribble. When the bus arrived an inspector with cap and clipboard called out: 'Contracts and war workers first!' Assuming she was a war worker, Ivy moved forward, only to be stopped and bade wait for the duplicate! Partway along the route she had to change onto the service bus — all this with gas mask, tin hat and kit bag! On another occasion, crossing Shap Fell, the weather was dreadful, with fog and sleet, and, this being wartime, the bus had little lighting. The conductor had to get out and walk in front to find the road. Ivy's problems may not have been isolated, for in 1943 a new weekly ticket was introduced to identify war-production workers. David Barnes's mother was a war worker being 'directed' to work for the RAF near Carlisle, this entailing a 1hr 20min journey to cover the 18 miles from Penrith, plus a further 20min to get to the base. Great excitement was generated when all this traffic resulted in Penrith's first double-deck.

In 1944 some 122 single- and six double-deck buses were provided for the Home Guard's stand-down parade. However, war conditions did not prevent the production and issue to staff of a fine brochure to celebrate the Company's Silver Jubilee.

Probably not noticed by hard-pressed staff in 1942 was the division of many bus companies in which they had joint interests by the Tilling and BET groups, Ribble becoming wholly BET. Of greater import to staff was Major Hickmott's retirement in 1944 and his replacement as General Manager the following year by Horace Bottomley. It was truly the end of an era, but also very much the start of another.

The very impressive Silver Jubilee brochure (*above*) produced in 1944 under what must have been very difficult circumstances, and (*left*) the personalised letter to staff from Horace Bottomley; note that Ribble is described not merely as 'one of the leading omnibus companies in the country' but as '*the* leading omnibus company'! (*both*) courtesy Kathleen Morris

Part Two: Ribble Supreme

7. Develop and Communicate Strong Beliefs

In best 'Catch 22' style, let's start off near the middle and work outwards. It is very tempting to call the 1945-62 period 'The Bottomley Years', for indeed he put a distinctive stamp on the Company. That would do a great disservice to the its other officers, who also contributed greatly, but Horace Bottomley was the figurehead. Ted Gahan recalls one day walking to his bus at Aintree depot and seeing the Depot Engineer in conversation with the General Manager. Bottomley noticed Ted and said: 'Have a good day, Driver.' 'I must say I was most impressed,' remembers Ted.

The back of a bus, Part 1: 1937 Leyland TD4 No C1736, one of the first with Brush bodywork to a style that was to be Ribble's choice for double-decks into the postwar years. *Colin Morris collection*

As a casual observer with some limited and specific knowledge and now delving deeper into the facts, one cannot help but feel that Ribble never really recovered from Bottomley's sudden death in April 1962. Other factors played their part, but the feeling of a symbolic disappearance of a father figure cannot be dispelled. In 1959 he was awarded the CBE, which gave R. P. Beddow, the Company Chairman and a fellow CBE, an opportunity to try and sum up the General Manager's contribution.

Starting work at 13 with Huddersfield Corporation, Bottomley progressed to Secretary to the General Manager, learning much about the growing industry. He then worked for United for five years

before joining Ribble in 1929 to assist Major Hickmott, becoming General Manager himself in 1945. 'Mr Bottomley and Ribble are synonymous,' states Beddow. 'His fierce pride in the doings and accomplishments of Ribble and its family is always evident. He believes that Ribble is best, and that is as it should be.' Stirring stuff. But what did he actually do?

In Bottomley's 30 years, from 1929 to 1959, the fleet (including Standerwick) had grown from 474 to 1,270. Passengers were up from 33½ million a year to 205 million, and mileage had trebled, to 52 million. The Ribble family had grown from 2,000 to 7,500, which is a lot of people. But Beddow was quick to add: 'It is in the best tradition of British business life that Mr Bottomley should have regarded the interests of the public as well as Ribble; his and our prime interest has always been that we should serve the public efficiently.' Not a bad mission statement.

Yes, but . . . isn't it all just words? Well, no; where we are looking we get a first-rate example. Let me introduce you to our new guide and source of quotes, the *Ribble Bulletin*, started in 1947. In the self-same edition as the Chairman's comments about the General Manager there is a three-page feature entitled 'Buy Britain's Cottons'. This extols the advantages of cotton and includes buying hints, answers to housewives' questions and photographs of rather voluminous dresses and frankly alarming trousers. But why? The article opens by stating that it was unusual for one company to sing the praises of another. 'Yet,' it continues, 'the prosperity of our company is partly tied to the well being of Britain's cotton industry. More than nine tenths of Britain's cotton goods are made in Lancashire, where the industry employs 250,000 people.' It points out that Ribble services radiated 'like a spider's web' from cotton towns such as Preston, Blackburn, Chorley and Wigan and depended on the support of spinners, weavers and 'kindred operatives'.

Talk about being the very fabric of the community! Ribble was certainly doing its bit.

◄ The back of a bus, Part 2: 1949 Brush-bodied PD2/3 No 2684. Comparison of this and the previous picture shows how body design had evolved but how similarities (such as the swept-back rear mudguards) remained. Note also the revised and simplified livery and fleetname style and the adoption of rear number blinds, as well as (on 2684) the big chrome rear bumpers, remembered by John Lloyd from his pram days on Merseyside.
Colin Morris collection

8. First Things First

Emerging from six years of war was painful. The fleet was pretty war-ravaged, and, whereas mechanically it was sound, things on the bodywork front were not so happy. Buses returned by the military needed much work before they could return to service. 'Wounds were being licked' is the charming understatement used by the Company to describe the task faced by its engineers. On top of this they had to lay claim to as many new vehicles as they could and were busily replacing the last petrol engines with diesels.

With the rebuilding and rebodying of wartime Utilities — and a rebodying programme covering 229 prewar buses and coaches — the Company began to meet its growing requirements. In 1948 it took the tenancy of a Barrage Balloon hangar at the RAF base in Fazakerley. Here overhauls, accident repairs and the backlog of body-maintenance work accumulated during the war were tackled under the watchful eye of Charge Hand W. H. Bell. Some 155 overhauls and 61 repaints later the influx of new buses allowed its closure, in March 1952.

Matters were little better on the Traffic side. Fuel rationing was still in force, and Government plans to rebuild the economy favoured exporting rather than supplying the home market, while the political aspirations of the new administration led to a new relationship between employer and employee.

On top of all this, demand was beginning to grow rapidly. Immediately after VE Day preparations were made to reactivate Standerwick, the company having been virtually closed down for five years. The bus industry has frequently (and not without justification) been quick to claim the effects of the weather, and 1947 delivered a scorcher of a summer, increasing demand yet further. Ribble's reaction was the widespread introduction of higher-capacity double-decks, which policy was not without its own difficulties. By way of an example, the Company had established itself as a major provider of services in the popular Lake District, and quite a few folk were keen to reacquaint themselves with it. One of the key routes was the main link from Kendal to Keswick, and Ribble was anxious to get double-decks onto it. Apart from anything else, the views would be superb. But the local councils, understandably mindful of their responsibility to protect one of the UK's most beautiful areas, were not so

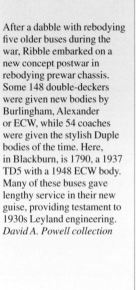

After a dabble with rebodying five older buses during the war, Ribble embarked on a new concept postwar in rebodying prewar chassis. Some 148 double-deckers were given new bodies by Burlingham, Alexander or ECW, while 54 coaches were given the stylish Duple bodies of the time. Here, in Blackburn, is 1790, a 1937 TD5 with a 1948 ECW body. Many of these buses gave lengthy service in their new guise, providing testament to 1930s Leyland engineering. *David A. Powell collection*

As well as the rebodying of prewar double-deckers and coaches, a more limited programme was undertaken with 27 single-deck buses. Burlingham provided 35-seat bodies, mostly on chassis new to Ribble but also, in a new departure, on some acquired second-hand from fellow BET companies Yorkshire Woollen and Devon General. From the latter came 214, a 1936 TS7, fitted with a 1949 body and seen in Chester Street, Bradford, in 1958. Urged on by inspector Bruce Maund, well known for clearing queues, Aintree driver Ted Gahan had set off on his first Blackpool–Bradford with little clue as to the route but heartened that he was being followed by another Ribble bound for the same place. Spotting a refreshment halt, he was pleased to see the other bus follow. Up came the other crew to say how glad they were that Ted was leading as they'd never been to Bradford before!
David A. Powell collection

keen. Rumblings of painting the buses green and restricting advertising abounded. Arthur Marston had become Engineering Road Inspector, and to him fell the task of driving the first double-deck over Dunmail Raise, the pass between Grasmere and Thirlmere. Aware of local feeling, a photographer from the local paper positioned himself at the top of the Raise and, more crucially, his car such that the bus had to cross onto the wrong side of the road. (Don't you just love the Press?) However, his efforts would ultimately be in vain, and nowadays the route offers one of the most popular double-deck rides in the world.

Given all this, Ribble must have been very pleased when, in 1946, double-decks were authorised for use on express services, sowing the seed for a most significant development on the bus front.

Other seeds had been sown. Just as World War 1 had produced vehicles and drivers, World War 2 produced a new breed of driver — the car driver. The Armed Forces, particularly the RAF, spent much time in remote areas where a cheap motor car often provided the only access to entertainment, any bus service having most likely been suspended to conserve resources. A habit had started. While the gradual relaxation of fuel rationing helped Ribble and fellow bus companies reintroduce suspended services, it also allowed greater personal use of the car. Oh dear, here we go.

It was new buses that were the key, and Ribble remained loyal to Leyland for its major restocking, although prewar bodybuilders Burlingham and Brush got a look-in on that front. Indeed, Burlingham adopted the prewar Ribble double-deck outline as its postwar standard. For double-deck chassis Leyland had introduced a new range, the PD; there was a corresponding PS for single-decks, but we'll come back to those later. Although fairly conventional, the PD was virtually a new model and went on to be one of the firm's all-time success stories. Despite needing new buses rather urgently, Ribble did not rush into it, taking 69 examples over the 1946/7 period. Much more significant was that 31 of these had highbridge bodywork — a first indication that the Company was moving towards a policy of using these much more comfortable buses where possible rather than standardising on the all-purpose lowbridge design.

The year 1948 was significant for two major events. The first was the fruits of the seed sown by the sanctioning of double-deckers on express services and an increase in width of vehicles to 8ft. On 23 June the Directors were treated to a demonstration run from Blackpool to Preston on what was called 'The New Express Service Vehicle', a Press launch following two days later. In truth the vehicle in question (one of a batch of 30) amounted to little more than a lowbridge Burlingham-bodied

The First Lady. No 2518, a 49-seat Burlingham-bodied PD1/3, seen here on (probably) 23 June 1948 about to convey the Directors on their first run on such a thing. Notice how relatively simple little embellishments make what is quite a basic bus look dramatic. The 'White Ladies' pioneered the distinctive, almost triangular destination displays and subsequently had their radiators altered to provide better ventilation. These 30 buses were the only double-deckers renumbered in 1950, this example becoming 1201. Fitter Edmund Chambers of Penrith recalls that people rode on them 'just to say they had'. *Mike Shires Ribble collection*

PD1/3, but every effort was made to ensure that 'the exterior of the vehicle leaves little to be desired in elegance and modernity'. Nice touches were a determined attempt to give lower-deck passengers a good view ahead and the raising of the platform to saloon level to allow a neat luggage compartment beneath. (What that must have been like for the conductor to deal with on a wet grimy day is another matter!) Transparent sliding panels were provided in the roof, which must have been very pleasant on a fine day. The extra width went into seats, not aisles, to prevent (as was delightfully stated) 'the overflowing of passengers into gangways'! Designed by then Chief Engineer Mr A. S. Woodgate, the double-deckers were the brainchild of Horace Bottomley and were intended for use on 60- or 70-mile express services such as those between East Lancashire, Liverpool and the Fylde Coast. Bottomley made no secret of their purpose in his notes about the launch in *Bulletin* No 17 of July 1948, issued, as always, to all staff. Firstly they were to meet heavily increased demand on such services; secondly they

were intended 'as a means of combating steeply rising costs, in this way assisting to provide an excellent standard of service without resorting to increased fares. To achieve this when operating costs have almost doubled since the outbreak of War (wages alone have increased by 75%) is making a valuable contribution to the National efforts to stem the rising tide of prices, because if fares were increased, practically every worker's cost of living would be affected.' Can't be more clear than that, and there's you thinking they were just double-deck coaches! Let us also dwell for a moment on the statement that bus fares would affect virtually every worker's standard of living . . .

On 24 July the first of the new double-deckers entered service between Blackpool and Manchester, the 'launch ceremony' of the 'maiden voyage' having almost been postponed twice: firstly the PSV licence for the bus was delayed, and then the driver failed to turn up for duty! The *Bulletin* report quips that he was no doubt suffering from 'stage fright' — no doubt his boss meted out a different sort of fright! A relief driver duly

took over and she was away, not without the final comment from the *Bulletin* that 'Others are being delivered, but unfortunately the flow is but a mere trickle yet.' Even at this early stage the vehicle was referred to as a 'White Lady', which prompted an interesting observation in the Engineering Department's section of the January 1949 *Bulletin* under the heading 'What's in a name?'

It explained that engineers tended to refer to buses by their chassis types, for example TD5 or PD2, whereas Traffic staff call them by their (as it is quaintly referred to) 'name on the engine', such as Cheetah or Titan. It was surprising then, the item continues, that a nickname should have attracted universal use, not only amongst staff but also among the public and Press. The piece concluded with a final accolade that 'even the most technically minded at the Central workshops talk almost affectionately about the "White Ladies" '. (Note the cautious 'almost'!) They must have been considered a success, for 20 more followed in 1950/1. Whatever in the war-scarred North West the sight of these modern, confident, forward-looking vehicles must have had an impact far beyond their limited role.

In simple but effective ways — notably the lighting — the 'White Lady' interior continued the impression of comfort. This view to the rear of the lower deck of an East Lancs-bodied PD2/3 shows clearly the rear luggage space and the level floor over the platform, again providing luggage space.
Joe Gornall collection

The second batch of 'White Ladies' — 20 of them, with East Lancs bodies on PD2/3 chassis — came in 1950/1. They were pretty much the same as the first batch but were of four-bay construction — fashionable at the time but not repeated on other Ribble vehicles. After withdrawal in 1961 no fewer than five of them went to Premier Travel of Cambridge, a classy operator no doubt attracted by the novelty value. All bar one served Premier for longer than they did Ribble, the last surviving until 1973. The former 1241, by now Premier 138, is seen in Bury St Edmunds in 1966.
David A. Powell

Cape Town' PD2 2647 of 1948 in typical surroundings, passing St George's Hall in Liverpool. John Lloyd recalls that these buses, unlike other Ribble vehicles, had green seats. *David A. Powell collection*

Christmas and New Year leaflet, 1950. *Mike Shires Ribble collection*

RIBBLE

1950
CHRISTMAS AND NEW YEAR

TRAFFIC ARRANGEMENTS

1951
★
CHRISTMAS EVE
and
CHRISTMAS DAY

Generally as on Sundays
★
SUNDAY & MONDAY
(DEC. 31st and NEW YEAR'S DAY)
Normal Services Generally

Workpeople's services and certain other journeys (chiefly early morning) not required, will be suspended

For details see booklets obtainable at Local Offices

Dynamic though the 'White Ladies' were, in terms of the staff it is arguable that the second significant development of 1948, the first-ever presentations of Long Service Awards by the Chairman, Mr R. P. Beddow, had greater impact. Certificates and badges were presented to 37 men who had achieved a quarter of a century or more (nice to see they weren't forgotten) of public service to a company that was only 29 years old itself. This became an important annual event, and in 1951 Miss V. Harwood and Miss D. Hayes of Frenchwood became the first ladies to complete 25 years' service.

Maybe Ribble had started off modestly with new double-decks, but from 1948 to 1950 it embarked upon a extensive programme to introduce Leyland's 8ft-wide PD2/3 model. Whilst still wavering over the lowbridge design, Ribble embraced wider buses with gusto, aided by the liberal attitude of the North Western Traffic Commissioners. Some 227 of the type arrived, most with lowbridge bodywork by Brush, Burlingham or Leyland itself, but included within this total were 42 highbridge all-Leyland buses diverted from an order for Cape Town and always known to staff by that city's name. Amongst all this two events took place, one being the adoption and refitting at overhaul of the distinctive, almost triangular destination box, pioneered on the 'White Ladies', that was to become so typically Ribble. The other was a partial renumbering, in September 1950, whereby the 201-700 series

was allocated to single-deck buses, 701-1200 to single-deck coaches, 1201-1300 to double-deck coaches, and 1301 upwards to double-deck buses. Although single-deckers were renumbered, double-deckers and those buses nearing withdrawal retained their existing identities. The old series had reached 2797.

Leyland's ability to match Ribble's double-deck requirements exactly was not repeated with single-deckers. A batch of 20 rather pretty Burlingham-bodied 35-seater front-entrance PS2/5 buses arrived in 1950, following 14 Tiger/Burlingham coaches, but the eyes of the Ribble management were turned southwards. To Birmingham, in fact. And not for the last time.

Poster from 1950 advertising for drivers and conductors. Giving a flavour of the times.
Mike Shires Ribble collection

A sunny Saturday 20 July 1963, and the penultimate double-deck bus in the old numbering scheme, 2776, approaches its stop in Moor Lane, Bolton. Really, this sums up a lot about Ribble, being a standard bus, of a type readily associated with the Company, working a local express service. An all-Leyland PD2/3, it was 13 years old and was thus nearing the end of its life but still looks immaculate. It sports advertising common at the time, trying to stem the already intensifying hæmorrhaging of passengers from buses countrywide. St Paul's Church in the background has closed, but the Albion public house is still very much with us — an interesting social comment.
Cyril Golding

Ribble's final half-cab single-deckers were big, heavy and had unusual sliding entrance doors. The Company's choice of O.600 engine and 8ft width, in effect making them single-deck versions of the current double-deck fancy, was likely the reason for the unusual choice of PS2/5 chassis. Despite being of obsolete design, arriving after the first Sentinels and within months of the first Royal Tigers, they put in a full service life. No 236, in Blackburn, shows that Burlingham provided rugged, good-looking buses. *David A. Powell collection*

Three of the 1950 PS2s would be beautifully rebuilt as tow wagons, one each based at Carlisle, Preston and Bootle; Pictured is BD1, previously 228 but originally 2778. *Ron Hopkins*

The second batch of Sentinels, STC6 models with Sentinel's own 44-seat bodywork, arrived in 1951. Delivery of the first six had been 'proudly announced' by Ribble in the *Bulletin*, but the 'incessant progress of bus engineering' meant that, 'modern and efficient as the original Sentinels were, room has been found for improvements'. Particularly singled out were the revised front and improved ventilation. Skipton depot, the one 'int' enemy territory', had one of these to cover a failed Royal Tiger, and Mike Lockyer remembers it as pleasant but a little slow for the tightly timed Embsay route. He thought the nearside suspension had a different rating from the offside; 'If one found an adverse camber or pothole, then Heaven help you, as it felt, albeit briefly, to be almost uncontrollable.' One was at the 1950 Show (as was Leyland Olympic 248), intriguingly bearing 266, an Olympic fleet number, as here. Maybe the Olympic order was increased, or maybe someone misheard over the phone, and it should have been 286. Either way, it provides a nice little mystery!
Mike Shires Ribble collection

BMMO (as this book isn't about that company we'll stick to 'Midland Red') had a habit of building its own buses at its Carlyle works at Edgbaston, Birmingham, which must have been a cause of irritation to Ribble (particularly as Midland Red, to Ribble minds, couldn't spell the place properly!). What was worse was that, following prewar experiments with rear-engined types (converted to underfloor during the war), Midland Red was able to churn out 100 of the underfloor-engined things in 1946/7, followed by another 100 to 8ft-wide specification and yet more longer ones seating 44 people, even adding insult to injury by lengthening older ones. It pulled the same stunt with coaches. And here's Ribble with 31-seat front-engined things and half-cab coaches! Leyland could offer nothing. Something had to be done. It was.

People must have hung onto the potted plants on Sentinel of Shrewsbury's stand at the 1948 Commercial Motor Show. Having carved a name for itself with steam lorries which — let's be fair — had underfloor engines, the company developed a similar arrangement for a diesel bus. Bodied by Beadle of Dartford, this appeared at the Show in Ribble colours — the first of six — and duly entered service on Preston route 109. Ribble engineers helped iron out initial difficulties, whereupon the next five entered service and a repeat order was placed for 14 more.

Did I mention that the 109 went past Leyland Motors' Head Office?

It worked. By 1953 some 140 buses and 145 coaches with underfloor engines built by Leyland were in Ribble service. In fairness, the Sentinels put in a full innings. In Carlisle.

9. Going Underfloor

Let's make no bones about it: the move to underfloor engines represented a major advance. Single-deck buses could now seat 44 compared with 31, and coaches could seat 41 (as opposed to 31) without compromising Ribble's insistence on comfort and adequate legroom.

The six original Sentinels had the honour of being Ribble's first, albeit seating only 40. Despite the arrival of Leyland's first offering — an Olympic that had been displayed at the 1950 Show — the second batch of Sentinels was warmly received early in 1951. But they had done their job; Leyland was now producing buses to the same layout.

The Olympic (the first of 30) was not what Ribble was looking for, but the Royal Tiger was another thing altogether, the Company ordering a huge batch of 120 41-seat coaches. The project which according to the *Bulletin* had cost 'not far short of half a million pounds' kicked off with a tour of the Company's

area from 23 October to 18 November 1950 by what Horace Bottomley called a 'near prototype', courtesy of Leyland Motors. Views of staff and public were invited, although in the latter's case this had as much to do with securing a holiday booking for the following summer! Even at this early stage, modifications had been agreed, and staff were advised of these so they might be able to answer any questions put to them by 'interested persons'. Already known as the 'Ribble Royal Tiger', the first one was christened at a ceremony at Leyland on 21 February 1951, when it was handed over by Mr H. Spurrier, Managing Director of Leyland Motors, to Mr R. P. Beddow, Chairman of Ribble. It was a fitting reminder of the co-operation between the two firms during construction. Mr Beddow commented that the vehicle would 'outrival anything placed on regular express work in this country'. Even Birmingham, he might have added.

Ribble's first Leyland underfloor-engined single-deckers weren't quite right. The Olympic was a joint production, MCW providing the body structure and Leyland adding the mechanical units, thereby creating an integral-type vehicle with no separate chassis. In fairness it was intended primarily as an export model, with a home-market version offered. Ribble's 30 were to the new 30ft length allowing 44 seats; they also introduced electric doors and a special lamp to illuminate the entrance. Such integrals restricted choice of bodywork, and Ribble also soon found that this arrangement did not fare too well on the stone setts common on Lancashire roads, which probably explains the switch to the sturdier Royal Tiger. Mike Lockyer recalls them having a 'no chassis under you' feel later revived by the National. The Olympics nevertheless led full lives in the northern part of the empire, 252 being seen here in June 1965 in Penrith. Beside it is Tiger Cub 457 on a short working to Fairhill which 10 years later would become part of the successful 646 town service.
Dave Cousins

A line of coaches behind a lady with a hat. In the spring of 1939 Ribble had undertaken its largest private hire to date — 360 coaches to take staff from Littlewoods Football Pools on their annual outing from Liverpool to Blackpool. The event was spread over two days but was not repeated, due to the war. Many memories must have been stirred when it was reintroduced, again over two days, on 23 and 30 August 1951. A more modest affair, says Ribble — only 105 coaches and 7,000 passengers . . . Littlewoods provided free travel, meals and reduced entrance fees to attractions for the (mostly) young girls and women, and Ribble worked with the Police to supervise entry to Blackpool Coliseum coach station to avoid disruption to normal service. 'We're not so bad in Liverpool that you have to provide a Police escort!' joked one young lass. This impressive line-up of new Royal Tigers is in Walton Hall Avenue, Liverpool — the main pick-up point on the 23rd. Two flat tyres were the only hitch, passengers being picked up within 10 minutes by another coach, while here were no problems at all on the 30th — a creditable performance by all.
Mike Shires Ribble collection

Extract from the September 1950 *Bulletin*, giving a preview of the Ribble Royal Tigers.
Roger Davies collection

Ribble Motor Services Ltd., Staff Bulletin, September, 1950.

THE "ROYAL TIGER"

An artist's impression of the Leyland "Royal Tiger" coach. The body design is that which is to be used for the 120 vehicles, delivery of which is to start in March, 1951.

Horace Bottomley mused on how he never became used to the idea of being a number during his service in World War 1, 'nor was I comforted at roll call'. This is how, under the heading 'Personality' in *Bulletin* 50 (April 1950), he introduced Ribble staff to the news that the new Royal Tiger coaches, were, starting at coach-only Manchester depot, to be fitted with Perspex plaques into which crews could insert their names, printed on pre-issued strips. The idea was that this official introduction would add a personal touch that would make all the difference, particularly on a long journey. Bottomley 'favoured the idea of a man being known by his popular Christian name, whether abbreviated, adopted or plain baptismal'. Billy and Wally here have charge of 781, the very first Royal Tiger, which also used the feature on its first run to Keswick. *Ribble Enthusiasts' Club*

▲ The Littlewoods outing on the open road. Nothing new under the sun — note the cycle lanes! The smart fleet, much of it new, caused comments along the route, being acclaimed by many onlookers as 'the finest fleet of coaches we've ever seen'. Return arrangements were for staggered timings, starting at 7pm. On the 23rd a heavy rainstorm at 6.30 caused hundreds to flock to the Coliseum; when it stopped everyone vanished until 8! On the 30th there were no such weather problems, no-one wanted to go, and a staggering 90 coaches were in formation at the station, loaded and away in half an hour! *Mike Shires Ribble collection*

When Leyland stopped building its own bodies Ribble had to look elsewhere, so the final 20 Royal Tigers had Burlingham Seagull bodywork, a type that seems to typify the 1950s. Burlingham was also local, being based in Blackpool. The last five were PSU1/16 models, fitted with air brakes in lieu of the vacuum brakes of the previous 140 PSU1/15s. Drivers complained that stopping Royal Tigers was not always that easy, so maybe this was a late reaction. Here is a splendid shot of 940 when new. *Joe Gornall collection*

The Burlingham Royal Tigers were luxuriously appointed as 32-seat touring coaches. The driver was very much part of the holiday, and those front nearside seats were doubtless very popular! *Ribble Enthusiasts' Club*

Following the official handover at Leyland, the first Royal Tiger, numbered 781, arrived at Ribble on a snow-swept 21 March and was prepared for its first run the following day — Maundy Thursday. On the stroke of 10 driver Syd Patterson and conductor Jim Cookson dispelled the curiosity of passengers waiting at Preston for the Keswick coach. They had watched photographers and Company dignitaries arrive, and now all was clear — it was a striking new coach. First aboard were Mr and Mrs R. Lawson of Fulwood, Preston, followed by 30 more passengers for the Lakes and four for Glasgow who, in the confusion, got on by mistake! Young Steven Hill from Edenfield was 'full of boyish delight' — what a start to his holiday! — and couldn't wait to tell his elder brother, an avid collector of bus numbers! No 781 continued its stately progress with excitement and explanations via Garstang (a mundane ticket check) and Lancaster to a successful conclusion at Keswick. By now the second Royal Tiger had been delivered, and this went straight to Bolton to cover 'Blackpools' and 'Morecambes' over Easter, and the rate of delivery was such that a considerable number were expected in service by Whitsuntide.

April's *Bulletin* gave staff nothing less than a four-page article about the concept, design and construction of the new coaches, a new conveyor system — the only one in the UK — having been designed to build them fast and cheaply. Over 10 and 11 April the first coach was loaned to the Lancashire Constabulary in conjunction with a Royal visit to the county; thus it had, as stated at the time, 'in some measure qualified for its title Royal'. The pride in these vehicles is self-evident.

By contrast with the debut of the Royal Tiger coaches, the introduction during 1952 of 110 bus versions was a pretty low-key affair. Basically a standard Leyland body was fitted, completed to meet Ribble's requirements; these included moving the door as far forward as possible and thinning the seat backs to 'a minimum consistent with comfort', to quote from the *Bulletin*. A major departure from usual practice concerned the driver's windscreen, which was recessed as far as possible to reduce interior glare. Shortage of materials was slowing delivery, but all entered service over an eight-

month period, at the end of which the Ribble and Standerwick fleets could boast 306 underfloor-engined vehicles, these accounting for 60% of all single-deck buses and 40% of coaches. Not bad, considering the first bulk deliveries had begun as recently as early 1951!

Ribble was unusual in building up a large fleet of heavy single-decks. The industry in general was calling for lighter-weight, fuel-efficient models, and Leyland's answer was the hugely successful Tiger Cub. Having already largely re-equipped, Ribble bought only 50 of these buses — one in 1953, the remainder in 1954. They were particularly fine-looking, with Saunders Roe bodywork of very pleasing and modern appearance, which made the Royal Tigers look a little dated.

The extensive updating ensured that no further single deck buses were bought until 1963, and when these came they marked another significant step-change. Throughout, Ribble had concentrated on the passenger and staff benefits of the new

underfloors. But Bottomley was quite open about the overriding reason. At the conclusion of the four-pager in the April 1951 *Bulletin* he had stated baldly that 'the new coaches (three of which will accommodate as many passengers as four of the older types) will assist the company in its fight against ever increasing costs, the task made more difficult than ever by the increase in fuel tax announced in the budget of 10 April'. However, all the Royal Tigers, Olympics and Sentinels couldn't avoid Ribble's first-ever general increase in bus fares, in 1951. Bottomley had held his promise for three years, but an April 1950 'bolt from the blue' increase of 9d (4p) a gallon, doubling the tax, coupled with other cost increases was too much, and Ribble had no choice but to follow the example set by most other bus companies. Immediately after the application (and completely unanticipated by the Company, after the savage increase 12 months earlier), fuel tax rose by another fourpence ha'penny (2p). It was to be a sombre portent for the future.

10. A *Bulletin* Bulletin

It is clear that, as well as resolving the physical problems faced by the Company, Ribble's management team wanted to foster staff loyalty and identity with a strong and respected brand, believing — quite rightly — that such investment would pay dividends in terms of quality of service. Key to the policy was the introduction in March 1947 of the *Bulletin* staff newsletter and, more importantly, its continuation on a regular (mostly monthly) basis. It was a major commitment. Paper was still in short supply, and photographic reproduction not very advanced. It is impossible to do justice to the 230 editions, all of which contain fascinating information giving a clear insight into Ribble. Many people remember them; copies still exist in households throughout the North West, often featuring a treasured article about a parent receiving a long-service award or retirement gift. The personal impact of them went far beyond the monthly doings of a bus company. They exuded *pride*. They still do.

Issue 1, boldly stating it would be monthly, set the format and is worth a closer look. The General Manager took, as thereafter, the front page to introduce it, inviting sports and social secretaries to submit news of their activities and inviting staff suggestions for improving the way the Company worked. He finished with the assurance: 'No harm can result from the advancement of a new idea — certainly not to the author of it.' Interestingly it is the only issue with the General Manager's name typed; afterwards this always appeared as a facsimile of his signature. Personnel changes, a reminder that the Company would collect staff National Savings and the result of a ballot over keeping the Company pension scheme (1,689 in favour, 981 against, in case you wanted to know) made up the General Manager's Office contribution. The Traffic Department thanked everyone for their 'Spartan' efforts (clearly our use today has become the opposite!) in the recent severe weather in what had been the worst February of the century, and those who turned up for work but were not able to were awarded an *ex gratia* payment to prevent hardship. There were details of new timetables, Easter services, excursions and tours, uniforms, the progress of a public-relations campaign ('For friendly

MONTHLY STAFF BULLETIN

RIBBLE
MOTOR SERVICES LTD.

No. 1.   FOR STAFF INFORMATION—NOT FOR PUBLICATION.   March, 1947.

"The Bulletin" Introduced

This is the first of a series of monthly bulletins in which endeavours will be made to keep the staff informed of developments of the Company's activities, of major changes or impending changes in personnel, organisation or procedure and of general questions where difficulties experienced might indicate the need for more complete co-operation on the part of the staff or better co-ordination between different sections of the staff. In short, the bulletin will be used amongst other things as the official instrument for maintaining a more regular contact between Headquarters and each individual member of the staff than has hitherto been the case through the more formal notices and (less frequently) through my personal staff circulars.

Within the limits imposed by paper shortage, the bulletin will describe social and sports activities of the various sections of staff with perhaps here and there anecdotes of special interest to those engaged in the road passenger transport industry. Secretaries of staff social or sports clubs are invited to hand to local officials of the Company any "news" items they may consider appropriate.

STAFF SUGGESTIONS.

I would like to remind members of the staff in all departments that suggestions for improvements in the working of the Company's services, in workshop practices and in office methods are always welcome. If any employee has a suggestion to put forward it should be made in writing and in the first instance handed to the district official in charge of the department who, if necessary after discussing the idea with the employee, will pass it forward to Head Office for acknowledgment and consideration.

In relation to all sections of the Company's organisation a good idea will usually stand the test of the following questions :

Will the adoption of the suggestion—
  (1) make things better for
      (a) the Company's customers, or
      (b) the Company's staff?
  (2) result in a saving of costs to the Company without causing undue inconvenience to either the Company's passengers or staff?
  (3) result in increased efficiency which would justify the extra cost incurred?

No employee, however new to the job, need hesitate to put forward a new idea, possibly fearing that it may not prove to be practicable. Sometimes an idea, not in itself good, can arouse other ideas which may be good. No harm can result from the advancement of a new idea—certainly not to the author of it.

H. BOTTOMLEY,
General Manager.

guidance, The Ribble Inspector' being one example), complaints and compliments and a report that 71 trainees had passed through the conductor training school in February. Interesting is that the period of annual holidays was subject to a ballot at Frenchwood, Driver Unsworth from Blackpool representing

staff. (The period chosen was 12 April–28 September.) A note refers to highbridge buses' being allocated to Merseyside, having previously only been at Carlisle, 'their bright colours and attractive advertisements a welcome promise of things to come'. Staff were encouraged to submit 'Road Anecdotes', being paid five shillings (25p) — a goodly sum — for every one published. Splendidly, it advises: 'If desirous of remaining anonymous, the author should give a *nom de plume*' … in addition to the correct name, of course, to get the five bob!

Two key features to appear were staff instructions and accident statistics. The former took two forms — staff circulars and staff notices. Circulars advised of changes to operations, giving the date and the depots involved, and were numbered consecutively. As an example, No 2764, issued on 3 February to Liverpool and Bootle, listed the routes on which highbridge buses could be used. The notices were more concerned with administrative matters and were numbered including the year; for example, No 24/47 of 1 February to Penrith advised on the conveyance of GPO mailbags. There was a fairly normal monthly crop of 22 circulars and 14 notices.

Accidents were classified by type, according to whether or not they had involved a collision. They were listed depot by depot and gave for each the number of miles run per incident, with a Company average. For collisions the average was 16,874 miles, with Morecambe (an urban depot) best, at a staggering 75,519 miles, and Skipton (a largely rural depot) worst, at 4,457 miles; for accidents without collisions the average was 39,793 miles, the highest mileage being a whopping 109,748, achieved by Bolton, and the lowest 17,830 by . . . Skipton.

On the vehicle front, the engineers advised on new buses (those highbridges again, including 2467 at Bootle, fitted with the latest Leyland O.600 engine, which Mike Lockyer reports was a 'goer' during a stay at Skipton), fuel cuts, Cheetah conversions to fuel oil and details of a new grade of engine oil. There were also some sports announcements and news from around the depots. A veritable feast!

The first two issues of the *Bulletin* ran to eight pages, this rising to 10 with No 3, which included photographs (of Drivers Rawlinson and Hoggarth, long-service men at Skipton, who had left to set up their own businesses — interesting), and to 16 (where it pretty much stayed) by No 10. Limited colour was introduced from June 1948. And the five bob worked; Driver Briggs at Blackburn got one for recalling a Stand Inspector wondering whether he had given the correct reply to a lady still

The first cartoons by Hignett and Harrison were 'Under the bonnet' and included 'Our nippy clippie'. This selection, including ideas submitted by staff, dates from August 1948. Note the 'White Lady'.
Roger Davies collection

'teased' by British Summer Time when she asked: 'Does the 1.25 Petre Arms bus still run at 12.25?'

A flavour of the times can be gained from titles of the General Manager's articles — 'Balancing the bus budget' (April 1947), 'Reverse' (July 1947), in respect of unofficial strikes that had hit the Company, 'Crisis' (August 1947), on driving techniques to reduce fuel usage, and, within the following six months, 'Wages', 'Courtesy', 'Accidents', 'Destinations' and 'Inflation'. You really couldn't say you didn't know what was going on.

A selection of *Bulletin* covers from the 1950s and '60s. *(all) Roger Davies collection*

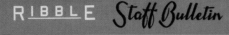

WESTLINKS

THE public and, of course, our staff are going to hear much about the "Westlinks Expresses" in the near future. The commencement on May 16th of a new Edinburgh-Liverpool night service will forge the last-needed link providing summer express coach service facilities daily from May 24th through from Glasgow and Edinburgh to the southern resorts of Torquay, Bournemouth, Portsmouth (for the Isle of Wight) and Plymouth via Carlisle, Kendal, Lancaster, Preston, Liverpool, Warrington, Kidderminster, Worcester, Cheltenham, also Bristol, continuing southwards by organised connections at Cheltenham variously to the South Coast resorts mentioned, as well as to South Wales including Cardiff and Swansea, also Weston-super-Mare.

Link services in the north will be provided to and from Keswick, Barrow, Ulverston, Grange-over-Sands, Morecambe, Fleetwood, Blackpool, Southport, Wigan and East Lancashire towns. For the coming season passengers from these link services will only have through connections to places south of Cheltenham—that is including the South Coast resorts—southward on Fridays and Saturdays and northward on Saturdays and Sundays. Bristol, however, will be served by the link services daily in both directions.

"Westlinks Expresses" as well as on the link services.

Through bookings will be available between all places mentioned and other intermediate towns served by the "Westlinks Expresses" as well as on the link services.

Our Company has always been well to the forefront in providing long-distance express coach service travel of a high-class order—indeed we run more extensive express services than any other operator in Britain. Our magnificent Royal Tiger coaches can be seen giving daily service to such places as Newcastle-on-Tyne, Middlesbrough, Scarborough, Leeds and (by our subsidiary, Standerwicks) Birmingham and London.

The operation of the "Westlinks" express system is the most ambitious undertaking yet attempted, covering, as it does, no less than 496 miles Glasgow to Torquay. Whilst it is true that for example the 10 p.m. departure from Glasgow, providing for an arrival in Torquay at 9.16 p.m. next day is something of a marathon ride, the return fare of 91/4d. (likely to be 92/9d. this summer) may not be unattractive.

Infinite intermediate possibilities are, however, opened up such as Preston (6.2 a.m.) to Bournemouth (7.55 p.m.) 53/3d. return (present fare) and Carlisle (7 a.m.) to Bristol (9.10 p.m.) 53/3d. (present fare).

I am most anxious that every member of the road staff and office staff should be familiar with the "Westlinks" operations so that they can give information to intending passengers about the facilities available and in addition ensure that as passengers are in course of making their journeys on our coaches they may be assured of the good service, accurate advice and prompt assistance which has built up our enviable reputation and prestige in catering for the long-distance traveller. For this purpose each employee will need to obtain a copy of the "Westlinks" leaflets when they are issued in the near future.

M. Bottomley,
General Manager.

A busy scene at the delightful
Ambleside bus station in 1953.

R.O.S.Co.

THE new organisation set up to sponsor the Safe-Driving Competitions in which all eligible drivers employed by the Company are entered year by year is the Road Operators Safety Council (R.O.S.Co.), not to be confused with the sponsors of the pre-1955 Competitions Ro.S.P.A.—The Royal Society for the Prevention of Accidents.

(Note.—To be "eligible," a driver must be in the employ of the Company on January 1st in the year of the competition and be employed regularly as driver for 44 weeks, including annual leave and public holidays out of the 52 weeks).

R.O.S.Co. will recognise all awards made by Ro.S.P.A. prior to 1955 so that there is no break in the awards earned in successive years by our drivers. In all respects, the new organisation will follow the practices of the old, with the one exception that the new rule adopted in 1955 by the old organisation in relation to convictions for speeding offences will not feature in the conditions of the competition of the new organisation.

The hub of Carlisle
operations, the Town Hall, in 1956. Here Engineering
Road Inspector Arthur Marsden would sit for an hour,
every bus would pass him and he would go to the depot
to report all the minor defects he'd noticed.

April 1952 with the header of the time
(a selection of the fleet), the launch of
Westlinks and the 'Ribble Family' below.

STIRRINGS

LATE though it is in following the dictates of the calendar, Spring is with us and the life-blood of every living thing quickens to its rhythm as the sun, the fount of all life on earth, gains in power and bestows its blessings upon rich and poor, strong and weak, large and small, with complete impartiality.

Ribble as it liked to be —
916 at Crummock Water in 1958.

DRIVE

IF we exclude chance—and I regard a football pools winner as a beneficiary of chance—there are but few worthwhile achievements in this life which do not stem from hard work and diligence. A man who wishes to do better than his neighbour must work harder and think harder. If success came easily and without effort, it would not rank as an achievement and everyone would become successful more or less to a degree influenced by chance.

Olympic 262
climbs Beast Banks in Kendal in 1958.

FREE FOR ALL—CHAOS

A busy scene
in Morecambe in 1963.

SUMMER

ACTS OF FAITH

The goldmine —
Blackpool, 1955.

Sometimes the bus
was only just there
— Horwich in 1965 ...

... sometimes not at all
— a Lake District
winter scene.

PRICES AND INCOMES

And who but Ribble would have
this on their magazine?
Well, it *was* RMS *Queen Mary* . . .

the mini-skirt has its critics
but—

New travel office in Grange

Ear-ring Crisis

Current issues were
tackled, like the
miniskirt in June
1966. The very
appropriately named
Wendy Gregson from
the Creative Arts
Department
concluded: 'If a
person feels she suits
a new fashion she
should wear it;
otherwise modify or
forget it.'

A cartoon from February 1950, celebrating the new width, a very telling one from November 1960 and a sign of the times (but with a message that is still relevant) from December 1966.
Roger Davies collection

Each Christmas edition of the *Bulletin* included a children's colouring competition, in two categories. Winners were announced in January.
Roger Davies collection

"AYE, THAT'S ONE O'THEM THEER NEW EIGHT FOOT WIDE JOBS."

GBell.

"It's a Company scheme to win back the motorist!"

"You really mean you've no telly?"

Cartoons, an invaluable indicator of social trends, appeared from August 1947, and from March 1949 until February 1952 a colour drawing of a 'White Lady' graced the front . . . except for December 1951, when it was an Olympic in the snow! There was a selection of articles on subjects as diverse as the origins of Christmas, moustaches and the Handlebar Club, Grasmere sports and a tour of the USA. There was a page for the ladies, recipes, hobbies (from collecting autographs to cord-knotting), puzzles, detailed reports on individual depots, departments or personalities, the annual report, road-safety hints, sports reports, industry news, complaints and compliments and the importance of correct destinations and smart uniforms. Each issue had pictures of five members of the Ribble 'family' from throughout the Company. Truly a family magazine.

11. Double Your Money

By 1952 there was a new Government, but it soon learned old tricks and imposed a further rise in fuel tax. In two years this had risen from 9d (4p) a gallon to half a crown (12½p) on a gallon that cost just under 4s (20p). This cost Ribble half a million pounds a year in tax, in addition to all the increased costs flowing on. The Coronation in 1953 allowed some cheer. *Bulletin* 72, like subsequent issues that year carrying a blue stripe on its red-and-white scheme, included a six-page article describing in detail the order and significance of the ceremony, who was involved, the regalia and a preview of the day, all with photos; bear in mind that not all that many people would have access to the new-fangled television.

A wage increase in 1954 cost the Company £120,000 per annum, and by the end of that year there were signs of growing industrial unrest. Bottomley turned savagely on those who spoke 'complete balderdash' about the profits being made by bus companies. The dividend paid to shareholders in 1954 — quite a good year — was a little under £4 for each £100 of capital employed. Large cost increases were anticipated in 1955, so an application to raise fares had been lodged. It is interesting to note the sort of things that had to be dealt with, all having a cost to them. A random trawl through the *Bulletins* of 1955 reveals traffic circulars for Royal visits to Southport, Blackpool, Preston, Accrington and Burnley, arrangements for Whitsuntide processions in Lancaster, Preston, Wigan and Bury (and consequent fare implications) and changes to accommodate the Preston Pot Fair and the Grayrigg Agricultural Show & Hound Trials, not forgetting excavations in Euston Road, Morecambe.

By September 1956 Bottomley was talking of a 'roundabout' of increasing costs, wages and bus fares. He explained to staff that it wasn't possible to forecast accurately how the passengers would react; they might pay up, walk or travel less; as a result that year's fare increase hadn't brought in what was expected, and, to make matters worse, there had been an appallingly wet summer. Thus application had been made to abolish workmen's fares. Then there was the Suez Crisis.

I tell you all this to put in context a pretty dramatic development. It probably defines the whole 'Glory Days' bit — my, didn't it all

In 1947 38 PD1As with Brush lowbridge bodies were delivered. By 1955 their timber frames had rotted — common with many bodies of that age — and it was decided to rebody 22 of them. Ribble went much further, fitting them with 8ft axles and units to accept new Burlingham bodies of that width. Re-engined in 1958 with O.600 units from withdrawn PD1s, they were virtually new buses; indeed, Ribble referred to them as PD2/3s. In this form they would last until the mid-1960s. No 2489 stands outside the finishing shop at Frenchwood, only its registration giving the game away.
Peter Yates collection

The new Tiger Cub model, again with Burlingham Seagull bodywork, met all coach requirements until 1958. Ribble clearly felt that the sleek side windows and bulbous screens needed improvement and in 1958 took delivery of 32 with a revised Mk VI body incorporating gasket glazing and flat windscreens. As the Company was probably Burlingham's largest customer this was understandable, but not everyone agreed, and the subsequent Mk VII was much nearer the original. All 41-seaters, they were ideal for excursion work, 999 here apparently having the Peak District to itself. *Joe Gornall collection*

Some photographers took many moons to realise that 'LMS' on bus blinds in the Manchester area had nothing to do with the railway but denoted Lower Moseley Street bus station. On the Friday before Whitsuntide in 1962 a bevy of buses wait their turn of duty amongst assorted staff and passengers. To the fore is Ribble 1369, a handsome all-Leyland product, carrying its 10 years well. Soon it will carry its passengers to Burnley, its relief being the sort of thing you'd more usually expect on an express service, a Royal Tiger coach. But this was a busy weekend. Those seeking the delights of Blackpool are offered a North Western Dennis Loline III with Alexander body, which, Paul Hill recalls, tended to emanate from Biddulph depot and arrive in Blackpool with strict instructions to remain there for five

hours to regain its strength for the return! If needed, this Loline will be 'duped' by the Ashton-under-Lyne Corporation Roe-bodied PD2 behind the Royal Tiger. *Michael Dryhurst*

There's a lot of criticism of the MCW Orion body, and, yes, sometimes it can look awful. But with exposed radiator and a decent livery it can look pretty darn fine, and here's how. Ribble went back to double-deck buses bigtime from 1955 until 1961. As Leyland had ceased to build bodies another supplier had to be found, and there seems to have been an informal understanding that former customers went to MCW. The design also satisfied the contemporary desire for lightweight construction, although Ribble's weren't actually to that specification. The first 50 came in 1955, half with platform doors, half without. Clearly one of each was registered first, so 1382 here, the second with doors, has the third registration number. If you get my drift. These were PD2/13s; later batches reverted to PD2/12s, suggesting the air-pressure brakes on the former hadn't gone down too well. No 1382 is seen in Accrington working a bunch of 'Padi-Accs' — service 274 to Padiham via Hapton. *Arnold Richardson / Photobus*

look fine — but underneath it was beginning to go wrong. But take heart briefly, for in 1956, despite its problems, Ribble reached its peak, running over 50 million miles and carrying 215,648,878 passengers. That is a very, very large number of people.

But back to the buses themselves. As revealed in Chapter 9, the single-deck situation was sorted, and a steady stream of Tiger Cubs was updating the coach fleet, but what of the double-deckers? Thirty last, final and finest all-Leyland PD2s came in 1952, and in 1955/6 some 120 more PD2s arrived. There was dithering over braking systems and whether to have platform doors or not, but one thing was clear: all would be highbridge. The Frenchwood bureaucracy was galvanised, and routes were examined in fine detail for clearance. A useful increasing of capacity to 61 was achieved, most having MCW Orion-style bodywork, arguably some of the most attractive of this controversial style, but 45 had magnificent bodywork by local builder H. V. Burlingham of Blackpool, its product just about defining the *genre*.

You could only make a step-change from here on; having recorded 'Help!' you had to come up with 'Day Tripper'. Ribble

was on the job, and a number of plots were being hatched. The first involved a rather curious bus working the L3 route from Liverpool to Crosby. This was Leyland's prototype Atlantean (281 ATC) which had the remarkable seating capacity of 78. But it was a prototype and featured unproven rear-engined technology. Although the extra capacity was possible partly because of this, it was due also to the newly authorised length of 30ft. Of course, you could do that right away with Leyland PDs. So Ribble did.

I bet many phone calls were made to MARTON 251, and the result was that Burlingham came up with a 30ft version of its double-deck body, seating 72. It is claimed there were concerns that the conductor would not be able to collect all those fares before someone slipped off unnoticed. So why not get the driver to supervise the door? After all, it worked with single-decks. Thus the PD3s were full-fronted, with forward entrance. In less than five years the seating capacity of double-decks leaped from 53 to 72, with the same crew costs. In the autumn of 1957 driver Bill Fergusson and conductress Bridget Loughran set off with

This is about as good as it gets — these 1956 Burlingham PD2/12s were absolutely superb. If you have to pick one, then let it be 1466; the author part-owned it twice, first in preservation and then as a hugely popular driver trainer at Maidstone & District. How nice to learn that it had been Aintree driver Ted Gahan's favourite too. It's still preserved, though not accurately restored. There were 45 of these buses, 40 with platform doors and five without — who knows why? The doors were notable, being of an electrically operated double sliding type housed, when open, in a compartment behind the rear bench seat, thereby allowing a wider platform area than did the previous folding type. It was called the 'Southlanco' door system. They also introduced strip bells in the lower deck. Pictured in 1974, 1466 and 1470 (the latter's windscreen surround surviving Ribble's painters' enthusiasm) are seen at Liverpool Pier Head as many would prefer to remember it, working some of those Liverpool services with a chequered history and generally loathed by Ribble crews! *David A. Powell*

A very early demonstration Atlantean, new in September 1959, Bamber Bridge 8 became Ribble 1966. Here, in May 1970, it looks every inch a Ribble bus but hasn't strayed too far, being seen on the A6 between Bamber Bridge and Chorley on the route from Preston. Horace Bottomley was very keen on correctly set blinds, and clearly his influence lived on. 1966 would be withdrawn in 1972, if you follow. *Dave Cousins*

1501, the first of 105 of these huge buses, whilst Leyland busily tried to perfect their successor.

A major strike in July 1957, lasting up to nine days and including two of the busiest Saturdays of the year, was one of the most critical periods faced by the Company — indeed, by the industry — for a long time and, with the benefit of hindsight, represented a watershed. As the year wore on it became clear that things were going wrong. Until the strike traffic patterns had been roughly in line with expectations, albeit showing a slight drop. After the strike revenues began to dip below 1956 levels, despite a fare increase, not aided by an unchecked 'flu' epidemic. By October passenger loss had reached a staggering 8-10%. A further planned fare increase was unlikely to yield its anticipated £3,500 a week and costs had risen by £6,000 a week to meet the wage settlement that had resolved the strike. In a piece entitled 'Repercussions' Bottomley warned: 'As a company we face a pretty grim situation.' The only course remaining (duly pursued over the following months) was to cut services — 'not a happy prospect, but then it is not a happy situation'. The accompanying splendid picture of Olympic 273, complete with conductor, passing through the wilderness of the Kirkstone Pass on a 650 to

Windermere, seems merely to emphasise the point.

In 1958 there was a concerted effort to publicise what was on offer and make it more attractive, emphasising the role of conductor/couriers in public relations, particularly at refreshment stops. A casual remark about more attractive uniforms had resulted in conductresses' being issued with air-hostess-style hats. Economies were sought in all ways; Bruce Maund recalls that every single light bulb used had 'Stolen from Ribble' stamped on it and that some wag remarked that this was the only company to put the General Manager's initials on its pencils! But the big one, trailed as the only way to keep loss-making services running in areas that would be deprived if they were withdrawn, was one-man operation. It started in the Clitheroe area on 9 August, being quickly followed by schemes in Burnley, Bury, Blackpool, Garstang, Lancaster, Kendal,

◀ 'Meadow Ville', no doubt in suburban Preston but indicative of many parts of Britain, plays host to an early driver's-eye view of boarding passengers on a new PD3 in 1957. They were probably all Ribble staff, so if one had nipped off without paying it wouldn't have mattered. One young lady gazes up in awe; why? The PD3s may have been big, but they were no higher! Note also the cleaner's switch, introduced on the postwar PD1s, not only as an aid but also to reduce battery wear.
Ian Allan Library

◀◀ A nice detail shot of a PD3 doorway. Ribble stuck to a sliding door with these buses, maybe after experience with the doors on Burlingham's bodies on the PD2s delivered the previous year.
Ian Allan Library

The last of the 105 revolutionary 30ft Burlingham-bodied PD3s, 1605, does the leavin' of Liverpool and the Adelphi Hotel for a run to Ormskirk in 1973. A dual-purpose Leopard follows in the then-new NBC livery, and Corporate Identity has caught up with 1605's traditional livery in the form of posters. Many of these buses saw further service, but not 1605; when Ribble finished with it in 1975 it disappeared.
David A. Powell

When new the PD3s were known to Ribble crews as 'Zetas' (no idea why — probably sounded space-age) or 'Sabrinas' (come on now . . .). Two cartoons from the *Bulletin* illustrate how they were received.
Roger Davies collection

"Vital statistics? Sorry! I was referring to the seating arrangement of our Sabrinas — 72-41-31."

"You're working one of these new Zeta72's, Frank. Here's your equipment — money bag, ticket machine, rolls, waybill and skates."

Following the success in 1976 of the flat-fare service 646 in Penrith, Cumbria County Council got carried away with the idea and stumped up to do the same in Kendal. This was a different game altogether, with some quite long bits of route, and soon proved the blindingly obvious fact that, if you halve the fares, you need twice as many passengers to maintain the same revenue. Many paracetamols and adjustments to longer fares later, it worked. One of those longer sections was the 546 Bowston–Helmside route; 1552, here approaching Oxenholme in July 1970, presents a very different aspect from the RESLs used later on this service and demonstrates that the big PD3s weren't always used in urban areas. *Eckersley / Photobus*

The Saunders-Roe-bodied Tiger Cubs were in the vanguard of OMO, 447 being seen on such work at Padiham in 1966. The 283 to Nelson via Fencegate was joint with Burnley, Colne & Nelson Joint Transport Board and representative of umpteen such arrangements. The bus may be a bit battered and the red not quite right, but this is a fine study of a Lancashire mill town. *David A. Powell*

It is said that the two daughters of Orm, the great Saxon landowner, quarrelled over whether the new church being built on their father's land should have a tower or a steeple. To keep the peace they built both, and here is the Parish Church of St Peter & St Paul in Ormskirk, the only church in the country so adorned. Makes you wonder if they quarrelled over saints too. If you thought your author went diving into the Doomsday Book or somesuch for researching a bus book you are mistaken; this — and a great deal of other fascinating information about the Company's area — could be gleaned from the Ribble *Bulletin*. Its compilers often didn't feel the need to include a bus as well, but as this is a bus book perhaps we should. So here, resplendent after a repaint in September 1969, is 1626, a highbridge Atlantean of 1960 and arguably the epitome of Ribble; certainly these buses caused a stir when new. Ribble found that the plastic supports of the front nameplate wore, causing the plates to fall off — an expensive and, no doubt, dangerous occurrence — so these were replaced by transfers, 1626 having the underlined name, a relatively short-lived arrangement soon superseded by the lower-case style.
Eckersley / Photobus

Ambleside, Ulverston and Penrith. Soon all the Saro Tiger Cubs were so fitted, the modification involving the fitting of a cab door incorporating a Syro change-giving machine and onto which an electrically operated Setright was mounted. A light was fitted for easy operation in the dark, while a yellow triangle in the windscreen encouraged passengers to tender the correct fare (albeit in rather small print). Many Royal Tigers followed and then some Olympics, conversions continuing until 1965.

A notable retirement in 1958 was that of Mr A. Webb, Central Area Superintendent, after 38 years' service; he had joined Ribble when it was 10 months old, having previously been Major Hickmott's batman.

The year 1959 was exciting, and, for the first time in a number of years, the summer was good, Ribble prospering accordingly. The 11th annual awards marking 25 years' service involved over 400 staff, bringing the total to 701. However, on the debit side the huge growth in car usage was taking its toll in terms of congestion — a situation made more irritating as buses were limited to 30mph even on derestricted sections of road.

In November 1959 the Company's first Atlantean arrived. Leyland had perfected its prototype, and Ribble had waded in with an order for 95, of which 70 would be to full-height specification, seating an astonishing 78; the remainder would be lowbridge 72-seaters. There were many new features, not least the two-pedal semi-automatic transmission, which just about made every other bus obsolete overnight. Drivers were given instruction and an opportunity to try out the vehicle, but it is interesting that it was emphasised that it was much the same in terms of wheelbase and overhang as existing single-deckers. Metro-Cammell, which built the bodywork, provided heaters for both decks, controlled by two switches on the driver's right. One marked 'warm' was for moderately cold weather; the adjacent switch, marked 'hot', was for very cold weather and activated a second unit on each deck. No doubt Frenchwood issued a circular defining 'moderate' and 'very'!

Optimism was high. In many respects passengers and crews loved the Atlanteans. The easy, single-step entrance was (according to the *Bulletin*) 'a boon to the old and very young

There's something about seaside resorts out of season, and there'd be even more if you could see buses like this. Nearside front window cleaned for better vision, Atlantean 1649 of 1960 prepares to enter Morecambe's Euston Road bus station in the early 1970s. It's on the 571 route from Lancaster, Ribble being responsible for the through route (the 'track'), the two local municipalities only getting within sight of each other at Torrisholme; this was a source of some irritation locally, particularly when they were combined into one fleet! The other bus is a Morecambe & Heysham Corporation Pennine-bodied AEC Swift, which even then was pretty unusual. No 1649 managed 15 years with Ribble — a decent innings for a type not without its problems. *David A. Powell*

One action that made Ribble a nationwide name was the production by the famous Dinky Toys of a model Atlantean. It came in green or red and, unusually, did not pretend to be a London bus. The green one had 'Corporation Transport' on the side, the red one the correct Ribble fleetname. At the time Liverpool's buses were green, and Meccano, the makers, were neighbours of Ribble in Aintree so that probably explains it. Here is the staff offer on the back of the September 1962 *Bulletin*. *Roger Davies collection*

Dinky Toys certainly sold more of its Duple Roadmasters than did Duple, the real thing not taking off. Standerwick had some, six passing to Ribble in 1963. Despite lasting only one season, Ribble fitted them with fleetname plates. 'Iron Duke' 1056 (ex-Standerwick 122) shows how Ribble registered its subsidiary's coaches in Blackpool and also the front-mounted spare wheel. Warns Mike Lockyer: 'Undo it quickly and it drops on yer toes!' *Mike Lockyer*

51

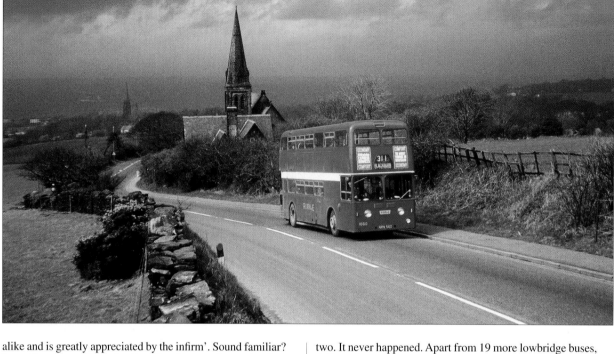

alike and is greatly appreciated by the infirm'. Sound familiar? Long-time *Buses* Editor Stephen Morris remembers using them on family trips from Manchester to Great Harwood when rides on Atlanteans were rare. Despite a journey time of an hour and a half they were perfectly adequate, unless the bus was one of the lowbridge type, which was too low for passengers to see out at the front and too high at the back. He recalls that they had a distinctive ride quality, 'with a gentle nodding motion which was really rather soothing, and with the engine burbling away at the back downstairs they were most civilised'. With the deep, rich East Lancashire accents of the crew, it was a most leisurely affair, the only excitement being going under the Central Station bridge whilst accelerating away with the characteristic howl as the bus reached maximum revs in each gear 'that would make the hairs on the back of your neck stand on end'. It's how he likes to remember Ribble — 'dignified maroon buses trundling along in an unhurried sort of way'.

Confidently, Ribble advised that, in later deliveries of the highbridge version, entry would be further improved by the reduction of seats over the nearside wheel arch, from three to two. It never happened. Apart from 19 more lowbridge buses, delivered over the next two years, that was it — that's all there was to what is regarded as an archetypical Ribble bus. The engineers weren't happy, and, as Ribble was a testbed for in-service trials of new Leyland models, they let their feelings be known. A further 141 PD3s followed, but, as Burlingham no longer built double-decks, all were bodied by MCW, still with full fronts. As ever taking advantage of any increase in maximum dimensions, Ribble saw to it that the last 36, delivered in 1963, were 8ft 2½in wide. At least the Atlanteans had ensured that they would have two-pedal control, with pneumocyclic gearboxes.

A quick diversion. Scout Motor Services of Preston, like Ribble established in 1919, ran a bus service from Preston to Blackpool and a Blackpool–London coach service, both built up in the 1930s and probably qualifying for Ribble's comment about a few competitors remaining after the 1930 Act. Relations were tetchy. Early in the war the Traffic Commissioner insisted on pooled resources, and a formal agreement was reached in 1941 giving a 60/40 split in Ribble's favour, with the Company carrying out clerical functions for Scout. Things seemed to

There's an old Cumbrian saying that if it didn't rain there would be no Lakes and no green. Well, it's doing it now in the early 1970s in Keswick, with 1756, a PD3/MCW of a type known as a 'Tank', looking very Ribble in the bus station as it waits to return to Lancaster. Just enjoy the reflections and look at those superb timetable cases, cost-effective plastic ones having been introduced in the late 1950s. The bus has the mountings for illuminated advert panels, but the less-than-dynamic advert for coach hire seems to be an ordinary paper one. Wonder it stayed on. *David A. Powell*

Rainy day in Carlisle — no wonder they never wrote the song. A couple brave the elements at the bus station in June 1973 to see where 'Tank' 1743 is going. The answer is Penrith, basically down the A6 via High Heskett, which, since the advent of Ribble's personal motorway, the M6, was a pleasantly rural run. Burlingham 1571 behind is on another fairly rural run, a short working on the Sebergham service, on which Audrey Mathews had got lost in the snow. These mighty beasts were now banished from city services by the onward march of OMO, as it was then. A very nice study of the two types of PD3. *Dave Cousins*

53

The Scout livery was very distinctive, and we can only hope that the wizards at the RVPT will manage to get their Atlantean into it for us all to enjoy. In the meantime, feast your eyes on all-Leyland PD2, DRN 365, complete with platform doors and lots of passengers at Starchouse Square in Preston on 20 October 1962. There's acres of anti-Olympic setts, a smart conductor and a wonderful selection of cars if you get bored by the bus. *Roy Marshall / Photobus*

The reason for the remodelling of Frenchwood in the early '60s in one picture: all 30ft of Scout S25 in Selbourne Street depot, Preston, in March 1967. Well, all right, the other 29 Scout vehicles and quite a few of Ribble's own contributed! S25 in the transient state of being Scout within Ribble before full absorption, hence the fleet number and fleetname. A 1959 Burlingham PD3/4, it became Ribble 1978. *Dave Cousins*

rub along, but Mr R. F. Shore, a long-time Scout driver, believes Ribble was up to its old tricks in driving others to the wall in pursuing its expansion aims.

On 5 December 1961 Ribble bought Scout, but, having discovered differing operating practices (such as running times), maintained it as a separate entity until 25 October 1968. Buses adopted Ribble colours and fleetname style, and frequent exchanges of vehicles took place. 'Thus Scout employees join the "Ribble Family", and we take this opportunity of extending a warm and cordial welcome to them all,' ran a piece on behalf of Ribble and Standerwick in the December 1961 *Bulletin*. Six Scout 'Old Timers' took up the 'Ribble Family' picture feature.

On 11 July 1961 buses 36ft long by 8ft 2½in wide were legalised. Ribble doubted whether double-deckers could be built to that length within existing weight limitations but felt there was some scope for single-deckers, to replace not doubles but, in certain cases, 44-seaters. It was a different matter with coaches, where the obvious advantages of extra capacity were readily apparent, and six of this type intended for Scout were delivered direct to Ribble.

Following Bottomley's death George Brook took over

With the Scout takeover in 1968 Ribble gained five Burlingham-bodied PD3s from 1958/9. Fit in nicely, you'd think, but they were never popular with Ribble crews, as, being half-cab, they precluded the conductor from chatting to the driver! Despite this the buses lasted until 1975, putting in as good an innings as did their genuine Ribble contemporaries. One-time Scout S21, now Ribble 1974, is seen in Blackburn in 1973. *David A. Powell*

It graced the cover of *British Bus Fleets 16* (eighth edition), this being devoted solely to Ribble — one of the favoured few to be accorded this honour. What a fabulous coach, thought a young Davies, and how nice to discover it really was. Ordered for Scout as S63-8, the batch was delivered to Ribble as 701-6. The Duple (Northern) Continental bodies — Ribble's first to 36ft length — seated 40 with a toilet and refreshment servery. Having joined the Standerwick fleet as 113 for a brief period in 1970 before withdrawal in 1971, the former 701 is seen in Stratford-upon-Avon on an excursion from Burnley — a journey reputed to have taken three hours with this machine, which was regularly quoted as having a road speed of 78mph. Just shows you how quickly manufacturers reacted to the potential of motorways. Drivers loved them. *David A. Powell*

Mrs R. O'Sullivan well remembers the friendly service given by Bamber Bridge Motor Services: 'Drivers would wait if you were running, and conductors put in a few pence if old folks, always called "Ma" or "Pa", were short.' On retirement in April 1967 the owning Prescott family sold to Ribble, which took three buses, two of which were formerly demonstrators. One of these, an Albion Lowlander with Alexander body, is seen as BBMS 6 at the Starchouse Square terminus in Preston.
Peter Yates collection

We will forgive the slight pinkiness, so well is the mood of the times conveyed by this photograph. Amazing to think that the Cortina evolved into today's Mondeo and that the Corsair was a bit of a styling triumph for Ford, if you can mix manufacturers like that. Bamber Bridge 6 became Ribble 1968 and had a new front dome fitted, no doubt to accommodate Ribble's blinds but clearly aiding forward vision too, if not its looks! The natives seem unimpressed that it was the only Lowlander south of the border badged as an Albion. Still, it is a February in Wigan, in 1972.
Dave Cousins

and continued the practice of writing detailed front-page articles for the *Bulletin*. In February 1963 he was able to announce a £1,135,000 order for 206 new vehicles for delivery over the next two years. 'Our vehicles are our silent salesmen,' he claimed, asserting that it was wise to replace old with new. There had clearly been some rethinking on the single-deck front, as 100 of these were 36-footers, 90 of them buses bodied by a new builder, Marshall — a type that would become a Ribble classic. It was now claimed they would replace lowbridge double-deckers, whose capacity they matched. Another change was the adoption of the BET Federation body design, Ribble having previously specified either its own or the manufacturer's standard. The other 10 were dual-purpose 49-seaters — a new concept for Ribble, which had hitherto quite happily used ordinary buses on express work. Mr Brook was making his mark! Significantly they were numbered in the coach series. All of the coaches were to 36ft length, the first having Harrington bodies, the rest Plaxton — another classic. Indeed, these orders set the tone for deliveries throughout the 1960s. Interestingly, despite the experience with double-deckers, these and initial subsequent orders featured manual gearboxes, only deliveries from 1965 having air-operated shifts. Orders for 1966 were of interest as they marked a return to 30ft 44-seaters in the wake of union intransigence concerning the one-man operation of larger-capacity vehicles. Some 55 'little Leopards',

Very Ribble! No 534, a 1964 Leopard/Marshall is the service car on the X14 Manchester–Morecambe in 1970, its 'dupe' being a Standerwick coach! This type of bus was known throughout Ribble as a 'Red Setter'. It is passing Robin Wood Mill in Todmorden, with Studeley Pike, a local landmark, in the background. This duty would have kept 534 busy from 5.50am until midnight. *David A. Powell*

The year 1976 was notable for its really hot summer, some of which the author spent looking after Grange-over-Sands depot. Could have been worse. That depot's, Kendal's and Ulverston's 'Red Setters', used on local services between the towns, spent most of the time in this configuration, trying to keep everyone cool. However, 530, seen in May, isn't on one of them; it's at Arnside station on the Lancaster–Kendal route via that 'bump' out into Morecambe Bay that also had the privilege of running via (amongst other places) Yealand Conyers and Yealand Redmayne. Ribble was kidding; although this was advertised as a through service, you had to change onto a 555 at Milnthorpe to get to Kendal. *Dave Cousins*

The final 30 dual-purpose
vehicles of the type introduced
by George Brook entered
service in 1968. The words
'classy livery' seem
inadequate. Bodied by
Willowbrook, they somehow
represented the peak of this
type of vehicle. No 923, a
Blackpool bus, stands in
Burnley with a backdrop of
snow on Good Friday, its first
day in service. It's working on
the Yorkshire–Blackpool pool
services, the 'Js', jointly
operated with West Yorkshire,
Yorkshire Traction, Yorkshire
Woollen and Hebble, and
standing next to it is one of
the last-named's rather nice
Alexander-bodied
AEC Reliances.
David A. Powell

Ribble buses were always a
good second-hand buy. If it
wasn't enough to find the
Company's coaches just about
anywhere, you'd also find
former buses, for many years
easily distinguishable by their
CK or RN registrations.
Leopard/Weymann DP 810
of 1965 didn't go far though:
with three others it passed
to Fylde Borough (Lytham
St Annes to you and me)
early in 1979, entering service
as 31 in May 1980 and
putting in two years there
before migrating to Scotland.
David A. Powell

Ribble's first 36ft coaches, not counting those six diverted from Scout, were 20 49-seater Leopards bodied by Harrington. From new they racked up high mileages on 24-hour-a-day Coventry–Manchester–Glasgow runs, after three years being overhauled and relegated to local express work. Shown passing the leaning café in Todmorden at about 5.30pm on a Manchester–Morecambe working in 1968, 708 would still not get home to Burnley before midnight.
David A. Powell

By the end of 1963 25 of the order for 35 36ft Leopards with the new Plaxton Panorama coach body had arrived. These were a major step forward, with long, deep side windows to 'provide passengers with an unimpeded view of the passing countryside'. The design evolved into an all-time classic very much associated with Ribble. Ten were for Standerwick, to supplement the 'Gay Hostess' coaches on London services. On this work they averaged over 3,000 miles a week and soon ran up high mileages. This is 730S at Burnley garage in 1968, about to go to Aintree to become a Ribble vehicle and calm down a bit. Note that front fleetname plates were produced for Standerwick and Scout too.
David A. Powell°

Ribble still had a requirement for low-height double-deckers, particularly in East Lancashire. Leyland had not managed to overcome the problem of uncomfortable upper decks in rear-engined types, but Daimler had. So Leyland imported some of its rival's ideas, and thus was born the PDR1/2. It wasn't a very happy bus. Ribble took 10 in 1966, fitted with this style of Alexander body that always looked a bit like some spare parts looking for a home. Here, in the late 1960s, 1869 enters Blackburn Boulevard on a local service, the B13 from Great Harwood. It is passing the offices of the *Lancashire Evening Telegraph*, since levelled to make way for the Market Centre. In the distance can be seen more traditional Ribble fare. *David A. Powell*

The former railway station in Southport made a spacious if quirky bus station. Getting out of it was another matter, buses having to squeeze out of a narrow exit road. And this is a low-height bus — another attempt by Leyland to crack the problem, the Lowlander. No 1863 was one of the 1965 batch of these curious Alexander-bodied vehicles. They were found only with Ribble and despite their looks were very nice to drive. *David A. Powell*

with Marshall bodies, arrived and, whilst pretty little things, came to be regarded rather as 'the wrong type of bus'. Also that year, for tour work, came 10 Bedford coaches; wrong type of coach, wrong work, wrong noise level, they lasted only three seasons. On the double-deck front, 36 of the 1963 order were the final batch of PD3s. Until the 1970s only small batches of low-height doubles would be bought; 10 included in the 1963 shopping spree were Albions. Stephen Morris, not realising the Lowlander was basically a lowbridge PD3, thought the world was about to end!

Stephen may have been right. Ribble as many remember it was now in place. The indefinable term 'glory' could be applied because … well, because it looked and felt like that. It isn't based on fact, it's a feeling, a 'feel glory' factor, if you will. But, as Adrian Jarvis puts it in his sister volume on *Transport in Liverpool*, 'it is worth remembering that a banana is not worth eating until the skin starts to go brown'. Maybe all was not well with Ribble, but it was certainly a good time to savour it.

The first attempt at a low-height rear-engined double-decker was the standard PDR1/1 Atlantean fitted with a lower body featuring a sunken side gangway and several rows of four-abreast seating at the rear of the upper deck, to permit adequate headroom downstairs over the driveline — not brilliant, but better than a full lowbridge layout. An early (1960) example, 1657 was nearing the end of its days — by which time it was one of the few buses retaining (by now rather faded) traditional livery, fleetnames and plate — when photographed in Blackburn. Paul Hill recalls driving sister 1675 — 'a flying machine' — on a last 125 journey from Wigan to Preston, when a couple travelling alone upstairs asked for the lights to be turned off! Leopard 541 behind displays the final form of the pre-NBC livery. *David A. Powell*

A Ribble bus: all the features are there — the distinctive lettering and numerals, the destination box and the fleetname plate. What more is there to say? This classic shot of almost brand-new 1954 in 1967 (if you follow) shows the bus at Tithebarn Street bus station in Preston. Given its healthy load it is probably reversing off before setting forth for Wigan (where its body was built) via Bamber Bridge, Chorley, Coppull and Standish. An attempt at a low-height design, the PDR1/2 Atlantean wasn't exactly one of Leyland's better ideas. The handsome Northern Counties 72-seat bodywork (this bus being one of six originally fitted with engine shrouds) wasn't that solid either, and sadly (for it looks so fine here) they weren't that popular. Despite there being only 15 of them they seemed to crop up over most of the operating area. *Peter Yates collection*

Leafy Northern heights with tree-lined roads of select villas, instantly recognisable as . . . Wigan. The last batch of 20 'Red Setters' came in 1967, returning to Marshall bodywork and the start of the single-deck number series. No 211 is here near Boar's Head running in from Preston on a service joint with J. Fishwick & Sons of Leyland. *Dave Cousins*

Ah, Real Wigan — the South Side, the Latin Quarter! In the shadow of dark, satanic, meat-and-potato-pie factories, Lowlander 1859 of the first batch has just passed over the Leeds & Liverpool Canal inbound from Billinge on a service worked jointly with St Helens and Wigan corporations. Chimney pots, leaning houses and a Hillman Imp give atmosphere, and you can't ask for a more accessible bus stop! The pot dogs were Araldited to the window ledges, and the china geese on the wall flew off as one of these thundered past! *Dave Cousins*

A lady looks for the door of a bus in Tithebarn Street bus station in Preston. Ribble took this over on 1 October 1926 with Pilot Motors and expanded it over the years until it closed on 22 October 1969 on the opening of the municipal bus station. In the building in front of the buses was a passenger waiting area with toilets and a tea bar serving tea in plastic cups. Beside a set of weighing scales was a ramp leading down to Lancaster Road with a tobacco kiosk and café where you could get snacks, meals and tea in proper cups. Further on, to the left, was the Ribble staff room; Liz and Philip Wilson remember the chattering and laughing and the smell of pipe and cigarette smoke as you walked past it. To the right was a furniture warehouse called 'The Galleries'; Liz and Philip never bought furniture but did attend the weekly comic-swaps there! There's a lovely selection of buses — Atlanteans, Burlingham PD3s and Leyland- and Orion-bodied PD2s, also showing that the elimination of rear number blinds was underway. The Atlantean nearest is a Scout bus in Ribble colours, as is the PD3 (S21) next to it. The lady's predicament demonstrates the problem created by mixing forward- and rear-entrance buses at nose-on bus stations. *Peter Yates collection*

Publicity for express services linking the Midlands to the Lakes and Scotland, issued jointly by Ribble (represented by its first Leyland Tiger) and Trent (a Duple-bodied SOS). *Mike Shires Ribble collection*

This isn't a definitive history of Ribble's express services. One of the key factors on this side of things is geography. Ribble was blessed in having the huge East Lancashire industrial region wanting to be linked to the seaside, including the jewel in the crown, Blackpool, not to mention the Lake District, Scotland and London. On 16 May 1952 along came 'Westlinks', an 'Express coach system' which (proclaimed the *Bulletin*) 'links up towns in Scotland, Wales and England in the West', bringing into the Ribble timetable such unlikely timing points as Treherbert (Bute Street). You just couldn't have been better placed. Ribble, taking a dominant role, built on this furiously, forging links with all manner of other operators both for joint running and for duplicates, its vehicles being seen nationwide. Paul Hill recalls Accrington Corporation, a regular provider of 'dupes' on the X60, having its newest buses delivered with 'ON HIRE TO RIBBLE' on the blinds. John Slater remembers the Rex café in Station Square, Lockerbie (a refreshment halt), having a sign proclaiming 'Reserved for Ribble and SMT buses', despite being well into Western SMT territory!

It was really the Merseyside Touring Co, taken over in 1930, that got Ribble on the right track with expresses. Until then it, like others, had used standard buses on such services, Merseyside convincing it to use purpose-built vehicles. Didn't always work: Bruce Maund remembers a letter of complaint arriving from a passenger who had endured a journey to Liverpool from Bridgnorth in a bus-bodied Cheetah. 'You should change your name to Terribble,' she asserted. This may have come about because, as Bill Jelpke recalls, Ribble tried never to refuse anyone, and last-minute ticket sales could cause an urgent call for a 'dupe' and sweet-talking a crew to stay on after duty. It was a vast exercise, the index page of places served in the Winter 1961/2 express and limited-stop timetable running to 66 pages.

Cop-out it may be, but I'm just going to say that at its peak Ribble provided 10% of all express coach services in the UK and was second in size only to Greyhound of the USA.

Think on that. But, just as with the Greek Islands of today, trade was sharply seasonal. Major Hickmott recognised this and as early as 1935 proposed a winter reconfiguration of coaches as more comfortable and private 15-seaters for all-year-round routes, to encourage greater usage at quiet times. His eyes were on such routes as Blackpool–London, on which an extra two passengers per trip would result in £300 extra revenue from each coach over the six months out of season, offsetting the cost of conversion. Neat, but it didn't happen. Still, the seasonal fluctuations, caused by the weather, were a constant problem for Ribble, and, when aircraft started to whisk us off to lands where the weather was not an issue and traditional industries began to fade, this side of the Company's business faced trouble. Ribble reacted with imagination and courage. Let's enjoy it for what it was and celebrate its sensational high-spots.

One thing we have to do is embrace the whole Standerwick Ribble thing. They were all one but were kept separate; Standerwick even had its own annual Ball. Scout joined in after 1961, but for our purposes let's think of it as the same thing but with different names.

So, motorways. In August 1958 Horace Bottomley wrote about their impending introduction. Express services at that time averaged 25mph. The Minister of Transport had announced that there was to be no maximum speed on the new motorways, so, when the network had been extended, an average speed of 40mph might be possible; 200-mile runs, such as to Glasgow, Edinburgh and London, would be achievable in five hours and thus come into the day-trip category. Bottomley signed off with the stirring cry: 'Motorways impart realism to yesterday's pipe dreams.' (More like a nightmare, if you dreamed about the M25 . . .)

W. C. STANDERWICK, LTD. &
SCOUT MOTOR SERVICES, LTD.

DAILY
JOINT SERVICE
TO
LONDON

VIA

KNUTSFORD, NEWCASTLE, STAFFORD,
BIRMINGHAM, COVENTRY

Single **18/6**   **31/3** Return

from

COLNE, Crown Garage	...	8-0 a.m.
NELSON, Tickle Street	...	8-7
BURNLEY, Cattle Market	...	8-18
ACCRINGTON, Edgar Street	...	8-34
BLACKBURN, Foundry Hill	...	9-8
DARWEN, Palatine Cafe	...	9-18
BOLTON, Moor Lane	...	9-41

LUXURY COACHES
available for **PRIVATE HIRE**

to all Social and Sporting Events

[SEE OVER]

H. 2,500. 5-5-51

But there was more to it. Readers will probably have worked out that the accelerated timings would mean non-stop running. Already Ribble had been complaining that refreshment stops were long, crowded and suspiciously pricey at peak times. Having identified the car as its major competitor, the Company was aware what a threat its flexibility was to this major part of the business. Ribble had already provided a coach station at Kendal bus garage, claiming this to be the first with automatic catering machines to speed things up. But think: if you provide refreshments yourself, served to your customers' seats on the move, you can avoid all this *and* have control of every aspect of their journey.

Enter the 'Gay Hostess' coach. This was visionary. All the parts came together — motorways, Atlanteans allowing 50 seats, with air suspension and capable of 60mph cruising, and the geography. If one clear example were needed of Ribble's ability to grasp opportunities, this was it.

Ribble made motorways its own. It provided guest transport at the opening of the very first one — conveniently, the eight-mile M6 Preston by-pass — the new era being launched by the Prime Minister, Harold Macmillan, in November 1958. On 11 April 1960 it was there for the third (a bit more M6), the Lancaster by-pass. Tiger Cub 1014 took some folks from a local handicapped home and 'Gay Hostess' Atlantean 1251 was there doling out drinks, snacks — and tours — for the amazed guests. These two vehicles were the first PSVs on the section, but already excursion coaches were leaving Lancaster full of people wanting to travel over the new road. It was opened by Dr The Rt Hon Charles Hill MP, Chancellor of the Duchy of Lancaster, and it is interesting to dwell on his words: 'May this road bring satisfaction and safety to those who use it. May they exhibit lane discipline and good driving manners.' Yes, well . . . In 1963 Ribble was there at the opening of the £26 million, 29-mile stretch of the M6 from Bamber Bridge to Lymm, the next day starting a 343-mile round-trip excursion to Woburn Abbey and a 331-mile one to Blenheim Palace. Bottomley's dream had been realised! Not an opportunity to line up with the brave new world was missed, so what of the second one, the M1 — the one in which Midland Red might be interested?

I can do no better than to reproduce (on pages 68/69) the excellent *Bulletin* article on one of the high-spots of UK bus legend! After three months' service the 'Gay Hostess' hostesses were selling about 100 items a day on each coach from their serveries. Based on experience, the idea went further into the 'Diner Coach', on which hot food could be provided, but the coach had to stop. This was an early form of corporate hospitality. A successful test run was made on 29 April 1962 from Preston to Shap, Ullswater and Keswick, with luncheon at Aira Force waterfall. It seems to have been a bit ahead of its time, but, curiously, at least one 'Gay Hostess', on withdrawal, was converted as a travelling restaurant, called the 'Upper Crust', touring London! Bottomley continued his crusade to allow alcohol to be sold on them, even appearing on television to put the case.

The success of these coaches seemed linked to motorways, and again Ribble's geography paid off as the M6 grew rapidly. They were not so suited to journeys like Liverpool–Bristol or Liverpool–Keswick, on which road surfaces and conditions were not so agreeable, and by 1963 all 37 of these trailblazing coaches, originally a joint Ribble/Standerwick product, were in the Standerwick and Scout fleets and used on 'Londons'. Twenty similar but less well-appointed Atlanteans came to Ribble for shorter-distance expresses, taking the 'White Lady' name of their predecessors.

Ribble expresses were a part of people's lives. John Slater recalls conducting an X10 from Edinburgh with a family travelling to Bolton. The eight-year-old daughter had never been to England before, so as they crossed the border John announced: 'We're in England now!' 'Doesn't look any different,' came the response. On entering Preston, the young lass chirped up: 'Aren't the houses a funny colour?' She'd never seen red-brick before. Rosemary McKinlay grew up in Liverpool in the early 1950s and travelled by Ribble to visit relatives near Penrith — first with her mother and then, from the age of eight, alone, in the care of the conductor. Leaving at 10.15 they would take strawberries or raspberries as a sweet and bought fresh homemade ice cream at Lancaster. Her mother used to say they could start to smile there! She finished her journey on the school bus to Millburn, having had breaks at Lancaster and Kendal. It worked in reverse. The folks in Millburn would send a whole turkey in a tea chest full of feathers by coach to Liverpool. Rosemary recalls: 'It was the start of Christmas to go to meet the Ribble bus for our Christmas lunch.'

An official photograph of a Standerwick 'Gay Hostess' Atlantean coach, taken when the vehicle was new in 1960 and used in contemporary Company publicity.
courtesy Ray Bignell / RVPT

67

RIBBLE
Staff
BULLETIN

NUMBER 130
NOVEMBER, 1959

ONWARD

UP to recently, there has been no legitimate justification for designing buses and coaches to achieve speeds in excess of 30 m.p.h. except insofar as this has emerged from a need for quick acceleration and the maintenance of maximum speed on upward grades—both calling for adequate reserve of power in the engine.

The opening of the new motorway M1 between Dunchurch and St. Albans, a distance of about 67 miles, has created conditions under which, for the first time, there is sound economic justification for gearing up passenger vehicles so as to be able to maintain speeds as much in excess of 30 m.p.h. as is safe and expedient.

Our congratulations go to our sister Company, Midland Red, to whom has fallen the privilege of operating the first really useful motorway service between Birmingham and London, a substantial part of the route consisting of the unrestricted-speed motorway. Operating turbo-charged diesel-engined 34-seat vehicles of their own design, proven to be capable of speeds of 85 m.p.h., Midland Red have cut about two hours off their former scheduled time because of the de-restrictions enjoyed on the motorway. In timing the motorway service, Midland Red have not attempted to maintain the maximum speeds of which their vehicles are capable but have contented themselves with an average speed of about 50 m.p.h. on the motorway which requires but little more than this speed on the road to maintain their schedule.

Thus, the new era is with us and dates from the opening of the new M1 motorway on the 2nd November, 1959.

M1 constitutes a little more than one quarter of the route of our Lancashire-London series of joint services with Standerwicks and Scout and the advantages it offers in timing cuts for our passengers will be available to them when some of these services are diverted to the M1 in the near future.

Tests on M1 on the opening date by our Gay Hostess, now fitted with a more powerful engine than originally, have shown her to be capable of maintaining an average speed of almost 50 m.p.h. on the motorway. With complete absence of vibration, an unintrusive and not unpleasant hum of the engine, the Gay Hostess is reported to have given a dream of a ride on the motorway and has opened up possibilities of serving not only solid but liquid refreshment whilst in motion.

We are encouraged to maintain our claim that for sheer luxurious comfort and a serene ride for the passenger, our Gay Hostess leads the field in public transport.

H. Bottomley.

General Manager.

M1 W

WE have always been in the front ranks of campaig for better roads for Britain and abreast of the tim on occasions a little ahead—in planning and i ducing new developments in our industry.

It was, therefore, with more than ordinary anticipatio with justifiable pride in achievement that in the even Sunday, 1st November, at 9.0 p.m., a small party left h Road Coach Station, Preston, in the "Gay Hostess" showing-the-flag expedition to the opening of Bri second motorway, the section of M1 from St. Alba Dunchurch.

The "Gay Hostess" was specially be-decked for occasion with streamer posters on each side indicatin outstanding features—Air Suspension, Reclining S Refreshments, Toilet. Other posters proclaimed that was "Britain's first really super-luxury coach" and slogan "Silent, Speedy, Safe Travel".

The party comprised two drivers, Denis Isles of Pr Depot and Joe Hamer, Standerwick's regular night se man, two courier stewards—D. J. Meredith and D Codling, G. Dawes, Traffic Assistant at Headquarters photographer, John Price, and D. P. Costello of the Bulletin team. Accompanying the "Gay Hostess" wa Film Unit outfit with George Bell, our Publicity Officer Joe Jackson, camera man, and in charge of the operatio W. G. Hunniball, Assistant to the General Manager.

An uneventful run was made as far as Dunstable with for refreshment at the P.M.T. Cafe at Stoke and Mi Red's Digbeth Coach Station, where the catering sta duty looked after us well.

Left: Mr. Ernest Marples, the Minister of Transport, at the o ceremony which took place at Pepperstock near Luton.

Below: At the opening ceremony, the "Gay Hostess" soon becan centre of attraction for the crowd.

e does it again

ere there

4.0 a.m. we were in Dunstable, seeking the advice of the
...rdshire Constabulary on how best to make our way on
... A6 south of Luton.

...r objective was to join the motorway via the Luton Spur
...e we had planned to team up with the Leyland Super
...t which, like ourselves, was hoping to be in at the
...ng.

...r map showed two possible bridge obstructions. One,
...he advice of the police we were able to avoid by leaving
...able for Luton via the small village of Houghton Regis.
... there, we made our way successfully into Luton,
...ng the second obstruction which is in Luton itself.

...m Luton, we proceeded south on the A6 to the round-
... at the Luton Spur. If there was to be any competition
...t place, there was no doubt we had won for no other
...e was in sight when at 5.0 a.m. we parked as near as
...ble to the "entry" carriageway. Some time later we
...ined by the Super Comet in charge of John Severn and
...an Darwin of Leyland Motors.

...er morning ablutions and breakfast on the "Gay
...ss," a sharp walk in the grey misty light of dawn along
...ile-long spur gave us a sight of the point at Pepperstock
...e motorway itself where Mr. Marples, the new Minister
...ansport, was to perform the opening ceremony at
...a.m.

...8.50 a.m. in company with the Comet and our Film Unit
..., the "Gay Hostess" moved on to the high level
...about on the M1 itself at Slip End close to Pepperstock
...oon we were safely parked on the north-bound slip
...within sight and earshot of the point at which the road
... shortly be officially opened.

Joe Hamer, Standerwick's regular night service driver who drove the "Gay Hostess" on the new Motorway.

We soon became the centre of attraction for the crowds assembling for the opening as they walked past us and on to the M1 carriageway.

—continued on next page

Below: This picture shows the "Gay Hostess" and the Leyland Comet on the Motorway making the run on the southbound carriageway.

9

M1 we were there—continued from previous page

Photographs and film shots were taken and we got our own pictures of Mr. Marples as he made his speech and again when he gave instructions by radio for the removal of the barriers at all the entries to the new road.

It was then that, with the Leyland Super Comet in the lead, we proceeded on to the northbound carriageway and became, we understand, the first commercial vehicle and public service vehicle respectively to travel on Britain's longest and newest motorway after its official opening.

We were first on the Preston motorway nearly a year ago and now we had gained another "first." Whether bagging "firsts" of this kind is to become a habit we cannot say—maybe the Lancaster By-pass will be our next conquest, who knows? We can, however, vouch for the feeling of adventure one experiences on such occasions and pride in knowing that Ribble (and this time, Standerwicks) was there.

From the opening at Pepperstock, we proceeded north on the motorway to Luton and then from Luton made the run on the southbound carriageway to the exit at Park Street south of St. Albans. Preceded by the film unit, more photographs and film shots were taken.

By now the traffic was beginning to roll on vehicles were entering the motorway from each end and at all the junctions and soon two magnificent coaches passed us at terrific speed— we judged it to be 70 m.p.h. They were two C.M.5's of the fleet of motorway express vehicles owned by our sister Company, Midland Red, making an inaugural run with a party of V.I.P.'s and representatives of the Press to start the first non-stop motorway express service, Birmingham to London.

The extraordinary interest shown by everybody in the "Gay Hostess" confirmed us in our view that as we should be only 21 miles from London when we left the motorway, we must go there, and we did.

We passed through part of the City and via the West End, Whitehall and the Embankment to Victoria Coach Station at the busy lunch-time peak period when everyone could see us —and people really did stare.

After taking food in the excellent restaurant at Victoria Coach Station, we left at 3.0 p.m., just ahead of the two Midland Red coaches, for the return trip.

With Joe Hamer at the wheel, handling the "Gay Hostess" as easily as if it were a London taxi, we reached the M1 at Park Street in exactly one hour—with our superior acceleration at lower speeds, we beat Midland Red by 6 minutes for this leg of the journey although there was, of course, no idea of a race in mind.

After about twenty minutes on the motorway with the "Gay Hostess" keeping steadily to its present top speed of nearly 50 m.p.h. and with only private cars overtaking us, suddenly two red streaks passed in quick succession. "That's Midland Red—that was" said some wit in our vehicle. They were going like the clappers of Hell—75 m.p.h. at least, and as steady as a rock.

Another half-hour of steady going, with the "Gay Hostess" behaving perfectly and providing a ride, the comfort of which has to be experienced to be believed, the cry went up— Midland Red ahead! And sure enough, there was one of the motorway expresses parked on the hard shoulder off the road with a front offside "flat". As we passed a cheer was raised in the "Gay Hostess" which quickly changed, however, to expressions of sympathy for it really was bad luck that when blazing a trail as Midland Red was doing that day, a misfortune, which is an extremely rare happening to a bus or coach tyre, should befall them.

Still, even good came out of this for the skill of the driver and the remarkable stability and manoeuvreability of the vehicle ensured safety and an investigation into the failure of the tyre revealed that there was no inherent weakness in design or construction and confirmed that the tyres in use are suitable for the higher speeds which may become general for coaches when operating on motorways.

Our first halt was at Midland Red's Digbeth Coach Station where we arrived at 6.20 p.m. making the time for the non-stop journey London to Birmingham 3 hours 20 minutes for the 116 miles (65 miles of it on the M1) including travel in the evening peak traffic on the Coventry by-pass and through Birmingham.

This was the test we had set out to make and it demonstrated clearly that the "Gay Hostess" will be able to operate comfortably in service conditions to the time of 3 hours 29 minutes for the Birmingham-London section of our London service routes including calls at Coventry and Euston.

A break at Birmingham followed by another at Stoke and with Denis Isles at the wheel, we were home again in Preston at 10.45 p.m., after 26 hours and a highly successful day.

On the Luton Spur in the grey light of a November dawn.

Left to right: Messrs. D. J. Meredith, J. Hamer, D. P. Costello, G. Bell, W. G. Hunniball, and the Leyland team, J. Severn and N. Darwin.

10

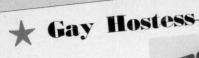

★ Gay Hostess

RIBBLE
STANDERWICK

A new style
double-deck luxury coach
for long distance
express services

RIBBLE
AND
STANDERWICK

SERVE
ALL
BRITAIN

DAILY
EXPRESS
SERVICES

The original 'Gay Hostess' leaflet and a
napkin depicting the Ribble/Standerwick
express network. *Ray Bignell / RVPT*

Right : A view of the lower saloon where there are 16 luxurious seats. All luggage is stored inside the vehicle, mainly in four compartments on the lower deck and in the spacious parcels racks in both saloons. The largest compartment is over the nearside rear wheel-arch — in this picture, to the right of the corridor, beyond the seats. Next to this compartment is the toilet.

Left : A view of the upper saloon, in which there are 34 adjustable luxury seats. Passengers who have already travelled in this saloon on trial runs say they cannot realise they are riding "upstairs." Due to the low-level chassis, special springing, the luxury seating and the absence of engine noise and vibration, the comfort and pleasure of riding in the upper saloon is far superior to riding in an ordinary single-deck coach.

Gay Hostess

RIBBLE and Standerwick welcome you aboard this fabulous and luxurious vehicle, one of a fleet now operating on our long distance coach services between Lancashire, the Midlands and London, the Lake District and London, by day and by night, on the established routes and on the new routes via the M.1 Motorway; and on express services between Lancashire, the Lake District, Carlisle and Scotland and to the West of England.

Built to carry you safely, speedily and in the utmost comfort, we hope your journey in it will be a pleasant one.

Revolutionary in many ways, these "Gay Hostess" coaches are unique in that they are the only vehicles of their kind in the world.

Looking forward in the upper saloon. Reading lights in both saloons are directed to each seat and are individually controlled by the passengers. There is also normal interior lighting with control for "bright" and "dim." An illuminated sign over the front windows indicates to passengers when the toilet is in use.

A smart bound volume was designed to sell the Diner Coach concept and included this shot of feasting clients. *Ray Bignell / RVPT*

These remarkable artefacts are original artwork created for the 'Gay Hostess' concept and were followed accurately by the real thing, excluding the ghostly Patrick Caulfield-type coves! *Ray Bignell / RVPT*

Standerwick 'Gay Hostess' 45 (formerly Ribble 1258) passes
Charnock Richard services, Blackpool-bound, in June 1969.
Notice how quiet the M6 motorway is (this would be about
4.30pm) and the lack of central crash barriers. The other vehicles
are interesting too. Chief Engineer Harry Tennant told Horace
Bottomley that the safest place on a motorway was the front seat
upstairs on one of these coaches. I wondered what the drivers
thought, their position being so different and so much amongst
things when compared with that of a single-decker. A classic bus
in a classic pose in its Glory Days. *David A. Powell*

The Atlanteans' replacements were Bristol VRLs, one of which is seen, in the
outside lane, passing Charnock Richard services, where, on 29 July 1963, the
official opening of this section of the M6 had taken place, Transport Minister
Ernest Marples telling the assembled throng that 'In the whole of the 21 years
I've lived in Lancashire, we never had a day as fine as this.' So that's why the M6
grew so quickly. Ribble provided the transport, of course. Irwin Dalton recalls
someone from another company referring to this outfit as 'Stand A Week'.
Not on this form! The ECW bodies were a one-off, even to the extent that
apparently identical panes of glass were of differing dimensions.
David A. Powell

A Standerwick doing what a Standerwick does best! Ribble was
proud to claim that its coaches spent more time in the outside lane
of motorways than any others, and here 1967 Leopard 881S,
working a London–Colne 'dupe' in June 1969, is about to enter its
spiritual home! Paul Hill recalls driving one of these on a feeder
from Knutsford services to Burnley with five passengers and
receiving £5 in tips. The following day he did a 'dupe' from
Preston to Scarborough and return with full loads both ways,
using an identical coach but with Ribble fleetnames. He got £2.50
in tips. 'Oh, the cachet of the Standerwick name,' he recalls.
So that's why they did it. *David A. Powell*

The new-generation 'White Ladies' were pretty fine-looking buses, and the reversed livery just seemed to fit in absolutely perfectly. Notice the nice touch of red wing mirrors. They didn't spend all their time on expresses, however; sometimes efficient scheduling had them slipping in a bit of ordinary work too. David Wayman, as a former Manchester driver, remembers driving Kendal's 1266 from Manchester and then doing a local to Kirkbarrow. This involved the steep sharp climb up Beast Banks. It was not aided by cheeky remarks about unfamiliar crews and 'old double-decks with armchairs' emitting from the lasses from the local laundry! When David had to pick up at the stop halfway up he feared that, given 1266's higher gearing, he might have to get them to help her move off! Fortunately she just made it. This one is in a classic Ribble pose, entering Preston bus station during the early '70s on its way to Manchester on the famous X60. Later in life these buses gained poppy-red bus livery and became known as 'Scarlet Women'. Happily this bus, 1279, has now been restored to its former glory by those splendid RVPT people. *David A. Powell*

Ribble coaches could be seen far and wide, and it is notable how, even outside their own area, they became part of people's lives. Betty Joyce Vines lived on the A442 half a mile south of Bridgnorth town centre. It was quite a feature of living there to say: 'Did you hear the Ribble go by?' (on the Blackpool–Cheltenham). She could still hear its engine as it speeded up, heading north after passing through Quatford. Her mother lived at St Annes-on-Sea and used Ribble to visit, the driver always stopping outside the house in Bridgnorth for her to get off. On a return visit Betty had to explain to a Ribble driver why she was photographing his coach in Blackpool. (May have been Ted Gahan — he did Cheltenhams.) Betty's son, Andrew, wrote a small tribute to Ribble, reproduced here with an early Panorama passing the Bridgnorth house and an Elite (954) in Blackpool. Betty says it 'brings back happy memories of days gone by'. Thank goodness she took the pictures. *Betty Joyce Vines*

29, Kidderminster Road,
Bridgnorth,
Salop.
4.11.70

Dear Grandma,

It is nice to be writing to you again; now it is getting dark and I sometimes see the Ribble bus go past with its lights on and today because the wind was from the west I heard the 1.15 Ribble bus while I was at school. It is still very warm and I am still going in my anorak to school. Tell Great ~~Grandma~~ Grandma that I got another Blackpool football player today to ~~stick~~ stick in my book.

From
Andrew

Good old Ribble

There was much excitement in 1972. New NBC
Chairman Freddie Wood was known to be a fan
of the US Greyhound operation and was keen to
re-brand the UK network. In 1968 the Scottish
Bus Group had adopted a quite revolutionary and
fairly American style of express coach built by
Alexander. So what better than to try it out (not on
the Scottish preference of the Bristol RE but on a
39ft Leopard PSU5), put it in the new livery and
bung it in that year's Commercial Motor Show …
and then give it to the premier operator of such
services? Thus we find Ribble 701 northbound
at Watford Gap services on Christmas Eve 1973.
Note the 'ON HIRE TO W. C. STANDERWICK' sticker
in the windscreen. We can but marvel at the
thinking that went behind the gash bits of tin used
to hold the fleetnames and ponder what it would
have looked like in proper livery like that
adorning Standerwick Bristol VRL 62.
(The VRLs looked dreadful in overall white too.)
Heralded as the first of many, this 46-seater
remained unique. *David A. Powell*

Perhaps as a result of the twin pressures
of a sharp drop in demand and NBC's
constant readjustments to the rapidly
changing market, some truly classic
designs and liveries had rather tortuous
lives in the early 1970s. Among these
was the 1969 batch of Leopards with
sleek Plaxton Panorama Elite bodywork,
of which 49-seat 966 is here in
Scarborough (where its body was built)
on an express service in 1974. After nine
years (the same lifespan as Leyland C67
of 1923!) it was despatched to National
Travel West in Manchester (OK, so it was
basically the former Ribble depot)
before being sold in 1981. Behind is a
Bristol LH of United. *David A. Powell*

13. Magical Mystery Tour

Ribble's policy that coaches were first and foremost for expresses in peak season tended to restrict the private-hire side of the business. All depots took some on, often benefiting from the advantages a double-decker could offer. The Company tended more towards showcase hires, such as the Littlewoods ones, which were aimed at promoting the Company as much as making a profit. It got into excursion work, of which there was a great deal in its area, mainly by acquisition; again, the Merseyside Touring Co was a major contributor.

Not all excursions were of the coach kind. When Bill Jelpke was in Carlisle in the early '60s Sunday Evening Mystery Tours, although declining, could still generate 750 people. Under Ribble's 'never refuse' policy these were often accommodated in open-platform double-decks, with conductors having to vary the itinerary to avoid overhead obstacles —didn't want *too* much mystery! The Sunday of Appleby Fair could bring 1,500 customers, buses being drafted in from Penrith. At three shillings and sixpence (17½p) a go it's unlikely to have been a money-spinner but was no doubt much appreciated by city and rural folk alike.

It was in extended tours that the Company shone. Again, these were an inheritance of the Merseyside Touring Co, upon which Ribble built up a hugely respected programme of high-quality UK tours. All meals were included, and top-class hotels used. The well-appointed coaches, with 32 luxury seats, were manned by a select band of drivers, whose names and photographs appeared in the publicity for 'their' tour. Philip Wilson remembers his Dad, George, a Preston tour driver, spending hours of his own time borrowing books from the library and surrounding himself with information about the area he would be visiting, so that he knew it like the back of his hand. It wasn't just amongst its own clientele that

Ribble was well thought of. Alan Connell, a tour driver from Maidstone & District, broke the rear lights on his coach in Lancaster. He took it to the local Ribble garage in Skerton, which didn't have the part but sent a fitter to a firm in Morecambe to get it, fitted it, and Alan was on his way. On his first tour, of the Lake District, Alan parked in Kendal depot, where a Ribble driver told him that, if he arranged a trip to the K Shoes factory, he would receive a free pair of shoes. Alan duly did this and had no need to buy new shoes for many years subsequently, still having a pair on his retirement in 1994!

One of the 1956 acquisitions, Auty's Tours of Bury, had a well-established tour business and was kept as a separate entity until 1959. From 1960 Ribble's whole programme was marketed as Kingfisher Tours. This was based on the Greek word for 'kingfisher' — 'halcyon' — made up of 'hals' (sea) and 'kuo' (to brood on), as legend has it that the bird lays its egg on the sea, which remains calm throughout incubation; hence 'halcyon days' has come to mean a time of peace, happiness and serenity — the aim of Ribble tours. Don't look at me — I'm just quoting the brochure!

Eight Lakes tour leaflet from 1928. *Mike Shires Ribble collection*

A small child appears to view the photographer with suspicion through a tennis racket. But why? This is a delightful fully air-suspended 41-seat Harrington Leopard of 1961, worthy of anyone's attention . . . as, it must be said, are the cars. No 1019 was photographed at Malham Tarn in 1967 on a fairly ordinary excursion. In the early 1960s Ribble had run a dramatic 'Wonders of the Modern World' excursion covering the M6, M62, Manchester Airport and Jodrell Bank. *David A. Powell*

George loading 1043 on the Southern tour. *courtesy Liz and Philip Wilson*

Tour briefing at Frenchwood. George Wilson of Preston is second from left in the back row. *courtesy Liz and Philip Wilson*

George with his July 1957 tour in Newquay. *courtesy Liz and Philip Wilson*

Kingfisher Tours brochure, 1961. *David A. Powell collection*

Driver W. Vivyan of Bootle on tour at Blairgowrie in May 1957 with a 1936 Tiger TS7 rebodied postwar with an 8ft-wide Duple body. *David Vivyan*

Tour hotel list, 1935. *Ribble Enthusiasts' Club*

In National Holidays times: 999 'Mk 2', a 1970 Leopard/Plaxton 36-seater, at Inverary in July 1976. *Roger Davies*

Driver Vivyan shares a moment with two passengers in front of his Harrington Leopard and . . .

. . . feeds the chickens! *(both) David Vivyan*

Michelin introduced a new coach tyre in 1963, and how better to demonstrate it than to buy two new 28-seater coaches to tour the country? By November they had done the trick, and Ribble picked them up at just about the same time as their own, longer, first Panoramas arrived, reseating them to 41. No 1060, the first of the pair, is seen in Penrith in June 1965. Useful little coaches, they ended their days in Grange-over-Sands, and just prior to their withdrawal one of them undertook a farewell Eight Lakes Tour. Both went to United for further service. They were registered in Stoke-on-Trent, home of Michelin's head office. *Dave Cousins*

In April 1958 Miss Pat Sanderson became the 100,000th passenger to book a coach/air ticket to the Isle of Man. This idea had been pioneered by Ribble in 1951, in conjunction with what was to become Silver City Airways, using the Blackpool–Ronaldsway air link. By 1958 more than 25,000 passengers a year were using it, including 13,000 who travelled to Blackpool by coach and on to the Isle of Man for a day trip. Not all passengers used Ribble, but it booked the largest number. The Company was also involved in coach/air bookings to Jersey and Belfast (via Blackpool) and Paris (via Lympne in Kent and Beauvais in France). Pat, a teacher from Prestwick, was an attractive 21-year-old girl. Aren't they all?

Ribble remained concerned about the growth of national and international travel. The Company realised that with its network of almost 40 booking offices — which were constantly being upgraded — it had an opportunity to break into the market,

and in April 1966 it bought the travel agency of P. Phythian & Son of St Helens, a business dating back to 1895, Eric (son of founder Peter) remaining on the board of this wholly owned subsidiary at Ribble's request. This acquisition brought with it ABTA status, Ribble being accepted as a full member in 1968. (I remember that, on my first day looking after Ambleside depot, the first enquiry I dealt with concerned flights from Frankfurt, while at Grange-over-Sands I once took a deposit on a Kuoni Safari in South Lakeland Council OAP tokens!) In a piece in a 1968 *Bulletin*, beneath a picture of sailing in Bermuda, George Brook advised that £1.5 million of the Company's £8 million turnover came over the counters of travel offices and encouraged staff to broadcast the extensive range of facilities on offer. It was a bold move, but, despite being a household name in and beyond its area, Ribble never became completely associated in people's minds with far-flung holidays.

RIBBLE Travel Gazette
1965

No. 5

RIBBLE LAUNCHES NEW WORLD WIDE TRAVEL SERVICE

Ribble moves with the times. Already the leading operator of express coach services throughout Britain, and coach/air services to the Isle of Man, Jersey and Ireland, Ribble now takes a dramatic step forward into the field of air travel. At every Ribble travel office — and there is one in most North-West towns — you can obtain free advice on air travel to all parts of the world, and arrange reservations and tickets for all the principal airlines.

YOUR NEAREST RIBBLE TRAVEL OFFICE IS THE GATEWAY TO THE WORLD

RIBBLE & BRITISH UNITED AIRWAYS

Ribble commenced its association with air travel in 1950 when it joined with the Lancashire Aircraft Corporation in pioneering coach/air services to the Isle of Man. When the Lancashire Aircraft Corporation was absorbed by Silver City Airways, the scope of coach/air services widened to include the Channel Islands and Ireland. In 1963 Silver City Airways joined British United Airways and the association with Ribble continued and developed. Now British United Airways operates scheduled services to East, West and Central Africa, South America, the Canary Islands, Gibraltar, Spain and Italy and to many parts of Europe. You can obtain all information and tickets at any Ribble travel office.

RIBBLE & BRITISH UNITED AIR FERRIES

British United Air Ferries operate between Southend, Lydd and Bournemouth (Hurn) Airports to eleven European destinations — Basle, Calais, Cherbourg, Deauville, Dinard, Geneva, Le Touquet, Liege, Ostend, Rotterdam and Strasbourg, and to the Channel Islands. The specially adapted Carvair aircraft carry cars and passengers or passengers only. Passengers from North West England can travel by the fast Motorway express coach services to London, Victoria Coach Station, where connecting coach services are available to Southend, Lydd and Bournemouth. This is the trouble-free way to the Continent. Full details of all Continental coach/air services can be obtained at any Ribble Travel Office.

THESE FAMOUS AIRLINES ARE CO-OPERATING WITH RIBBLE TO PROVIDE A WORLD WIDE TRAVEL INFORMATION SERVICE

AER LINGUS
AIR FRANCE
AIR INDIA
ALITALIA ITALIAN AIRLINES
BRITISH EAGLE
B.E.A.
B.O.A.C.
CAMBRIAN AIRWAYS
DAN-AIR
EL-AL ISRAEL AIRLINES
IBERIA AIRLINES OF SPAIN

K L M ROYAL DUTCH AIRLINES
LUFTHANSA GERMAN AIRLINES
QANTAS EMPIRE AIRWAYS
SABENA BELGIAN AIRLINES
SCANDINAVIAN AIRLINES (S.A.S.)
SWISSAIR
TRANS WORLD AIRWAYS

BRITISH UNITED JETS . .

British United is the first airline in the World to introduce two types of 'second generation' jets into service; these are the superb rear-engined BAC One-Eleven and the VC 10, the quietest and smoothest aircraft in the World.

Below : A B.A.C. One Eleven Jet takes off for Gibraltar

An example of a refurbished travel shop — the Preston Travel Corner in 1970.
Roger Davies collection

Clear indication of Ribble's determination to be part of the wider travel trade — a *Travel Gazette* from 1965.
Mike Shires Ribble collection

14. Frenchwood

It is a little-known fact that Ribble was a massive property owner and lessor. During its history, throughout its area, it was responsible for 80 garages, 73 offices, 12 bus stations and 19 residential sites. The latter ranged from individual houses, many in Preston, to 70 houses and three shops on the Northway Estate in Maghull and even included seven hotels and a shop in Tyldesley Road, Blackpool; much of this would be sold off in the desperate years of the late 1960s and early '70s. In addition a further 140 properties were acquired but not used. One of the most interesting was the Coliseum coach station in Blackpool, administered by Blackpool Omnibus Stations Ltd, with 50% of the capital put in by Ribble and the rest by the North Western, Yorkshire Traction, Yorkshire Woollen, Hebble, East Yorkshire and West Yorkshire companies, although it counted as a Ribble subsidiary. All this required maintaining and updating, both to improve working conditions and to match Ribble's travel-trade aspirations, so the Architect's Department was kept busy.

King of the buildings was Frenchwood Head Office, an imposing structure. On ascending two flights of stairs you passed through double swing doors into the reception area. In front of you was the staircase to the first floor; if you were early enough you would see the banisters getting their daily polish. As well as accommodating the senior officers, the first floor was home to the Architects, Engineering, Wages and Accounts departments. Mr R. Fitch, a member of the Accounts staff and responsible for pensions and the sickness fund from 1959 until 1967, recalls that twice a day a canteen lady would appear, to sell confectionery and cigarettes. She had competition from 'Harry Blackburn's Shop' — the top drawer of his desk — which did brisker business than his real shop in New Hall Lane. Joe Gornall says everyone knew about Harry's shop, including senior management 'who alternated between closing it down (it often operated undercover for a while) and sending for supplies'. Another task performed by the Accounts Department arose from the Company's participation in joint services, most of which were established in the '30s. Both stage and express, and shared with a plethora of other operators, these were a feature of Ribble and ranged from the huge Lancashire Scottish pool to arrangements with Pennine Motors of Gargrave

Frenchwood . . .
Roger Davies collection

. . . and a map produced for the 1982 Open Day, showing the layout.
Ron Hopkins

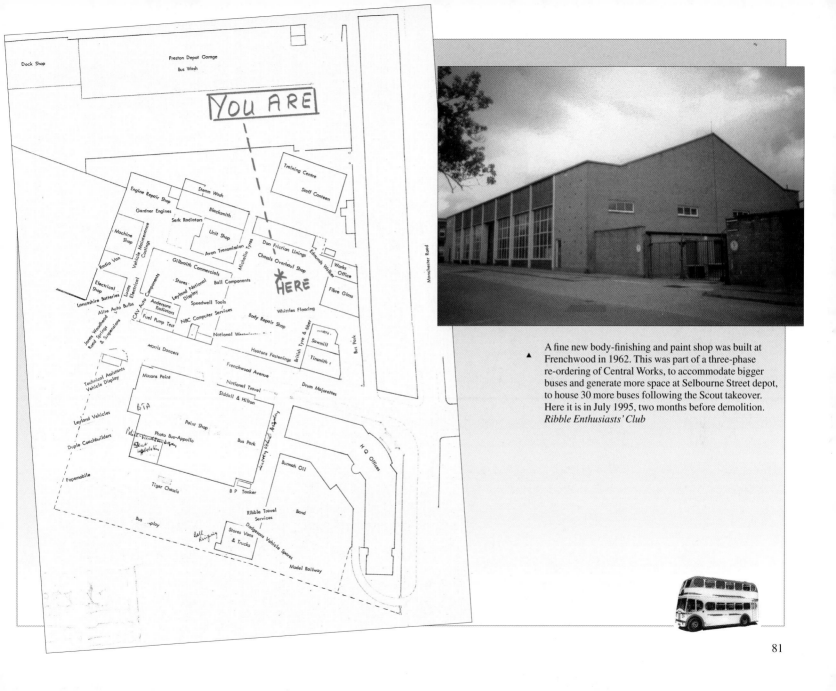

Dock Shop

Preston Depot Garage

Bus Wash

YOU ARE

Training Centre

Staff Canteen

Engine Repair Shop

Steam Wash

Gardner Engines

Blacksmith

Serk Radiators

Unit Shop

Machine Shop

Avon Transmission

Don Friction Linings

Michelin Tyres

Edmunds Walker

Works Office

Vehicle Maintenance Castings

Chassis Overhaul Shop

HERE

Radio Van

Gilbraith Commercials

Stores

Ball Components

Electrical Shop

Lucas Electrical

Leyland National Display

Fibre Glass

Components

Andersons Radiators

Speedwell Tools

Lancashire Batteries

Allite Auto Bulbs

ICAV Auto

NBC Computer Services

Whittles Flooring

Jones Woodhead Road Springs & Suspensions

Fuel Pump Test

Body Repair Shop

National Westminster

Morris Dancers

British Tyre & ...ber

Sawmill

Heatons Fastenings

Tinsmith

Bus Park

Technical Assistants Vehicle Display

Masons Paint

Frenchwood Avenue

Drum Majorettes

National Travel

BTA

Siddall & Hilton

Leyland Vehicles

Paint Shop

Photo Bus-Appollo

Bus Park

Duple Coachbuilders

H Q Offices

Papermobile

Tiger Chassis

B P Tanker

Burmah Oil

Ribble Travel Services

Band

Bus ...play

Dodgsons Vehicle Spares

Stores Vans & Trucks

Model Railway

Manchester Road

A fine new body-finishing and paint shop was built at Frenchwood in 1962. This was part of a three-phase re-ordering of Central Works, to accommodate bigger buses and generate more space at Selbourne Street depot, to house 30 more buses following the Scout takeover. Here it is in July 1995, two months before demolition. *Ribble Enthusiasts' Club*

Euston Road bus station, Morecambe, came into use in 1936 on railway land. The shelters and platforms were added postwar, and in 1953 the freehold was bought by Ribble for £9,800. Here it is shortly afterwards, in June 1954. Terminating buses dropped off outside, pulling around to load up. *Ribble Enthusiasts' Club*

Liverpool has many famous sites. Between two of them — Lime Street station and the Adelphi Hotel — Ribble built, at a cost of £190,000, the Skelhorne Street two-level bus/coach station, the coaches being upstairs, the buses below. Proudly flying the flag, this is the coach entrance in Hilbre Street in July 1960. No fewer than six municipal leaders — the mayors of Liverpool, Crosby and Bootle and the council chairmen of Formby, Ormskirk, and Litherland — were given a tour of inspection along with senior Ribble folk and PD3 No 1558. The building was pronounced worthy of Ribble and a credit to Liverpool. Senior Police officers also attended, and, following luncheon at the Adelphi, Ribble Chairman R. P. Beddow took the opportunity to regale them on the 'menace to the smooth working of public services' by careless car parking and how it had to be checked 'from the earliest stages'!
Ribble Enthusiasts' Club

over the Lancaster–Skipton route, and no two were the same. Each involved meticulous procedures for mileage- and revenue-balancing, known in intimate detail by Jack Thompson, who spent his entire working life thus employed at Frenchwood. Also upstairs was the mail room, with two staff sorting post, and the typing pool of 15-20 ladies strictly allocated to various departments and forbidden to deal in matters from another section. The Traffic Department was downstairs, and John Slater remembers that mere traffic clerks were not allowed upstairs without special permission. If a rush typing job was needed, agreement had to be obtained from the typing supervisor and a traffic clerk despatched with strict instructions not to talk to or acknowledge the junior typists!

Within the Engineering Department, with the central works next door and across the road, could be found another of Ribble's key characters. Unlike others we have met, Chief Engineer Harry Tennant was very low-profile, but his influence on Ribble was immense, and, having come from Leyland Motors, he maintained the link between manufacturer and operator. Ron Hopkins (himself a major part of the Ribble story,

putting in 51 years) recalls Tennant as a very private person. 'He was a strict disciplinarian, always used surnames and insisted on suits and ties. On Saturdays you could wear slacks and a sports coat but still had to have a tie. He liked new initiatives, new ideas, but you had to justify them, and he had no time for "yes" men. He was an absolute perfectionist; we used to go to see the first of a new batch of buses, and if it was not right he wouldn't allow it to be delivered. He may have caused frustration, but I believe the manufacturer's product was better as a result.' Tennant was also a stickler for timekeeping: on one occasion, having kept him waiting for 10 minutes, the managing director of a major coachbuilder had to run down the street to ask him to return! 'He was a great influence on me,' says Ron; 'he was a great man to listen to and follow.' There is no doubt that, if Bottomley had the grand ideas, Tennant and his team, whom he consulted in detail, made it happen. 'The "Gay Hostess" project was a case in point,' remembers Ron; 'we were at the cutting edge of development with those.'

The vast centralised Traffic Department dealt with all scheduling matters, its clerks quite likely never having visited

Talking to a 30-year-service conductor, Company Architect Cecil Quinn opined that the man had not progressed, not even having made Inspector. 'You've not gone so far yourself,' came the reply; '30 years and you're still the Architect!' This was a tale told by Cecil himself, a 'Quinnism' for which he was renowned. He had the reputation of being the most jovial, bright and breezy of the management team, being always ready with a smile, joke or good story. His finest achievement, he felt, was Aintree depot, a major suburban postwar development designed to meet the needs of the expansion of Liverpool. This was his retirement presentation, on 31 March 1960. Starting with the man with the moustache and moving clockwise, are: A. B. Dodd (the new Company Architect), J. P. Senior (Assistant General Manager), Mrs Waller, L. Waller (Traffic Manager), Mrs Tennant, Mr H. Tennant (Chief Engineer), H. W. Miler (Company Secretary), Mrs Miller, C. D. Quinn (outgoing Company Architect), Mrs Quinn, H. Bottomley (General Manager), Mrs Bottomley, F. A. Dickinson (a former Traffic Manager), Mrs Hunniball, W. G. Hunniball (assistant to the General Manager) and Mrs Dodd. *Ribble Enthusiasts' Club*

the places to which they sent buses and crews. Fares were a complex business, given the number of other companies running alongside Ribble with which these had to be aligned — so much so that in some areas Ribble's own fares were never charged. The Traffic Department was also the home of a strange tongue (though the mists of time obscure its origins), whereby Ribble referred to its depots by a letter code, the first (in Park Road, Preston) being AA, the second (Selbourne Street, Preston) AB, and so on. Everything — running sheets, bus workings, timetables, faretables — carried these codes; even the buses had it in a third tax disc. It was distinctively 'Ribble', and learning the lingo was a vital prerequisite for engaging in conversation. It was in the running-sheet system that Ribble was at its idiosyncratic best. I was once asked if I had come across this system elsewhere, to which I replied that I thought it unique. 'Ah, everyone else is out of line then!' came the response.

Here too was advance booking control for expresses —

a bit hit-and-miss, as not everyone booked in advance. Joe Gornall remembers experience coming into it: 'How many ont' Glasgow on Friday?' 'Thirty.' 'I'll put three coaches on then, with a standby at Preston.' Also controlled here were tours, excursions and private hires, including 'railway jobs' for train replacement and staff transport during engineering works. Behind the building was 'George Brook's Green'. This had been laid at his suggestion to replace an area of air-raid shelters, and the man himself would get upset when during summer staff took to basking on it!

Shortly after joining Ribble as General Manager, Irwin Dalton left his wood-panelled office for a few hours, on his return finding an old file on his otherwise clear desk. It was Horace Bottomley's, containing his advice on looking after the staff, and Irwin ambled out to thank his secretary for digging it out. 'Wasn't me,' she said; 'in fact I've been here all the time, and no one has been in your office.'

Travelling the Company's area, the Architects' Department needed a mobile base from which to work, a role fulfilled by a succession of former service buses. The one-time 2329, an all-Leyland TD7, is seen near Moor Lane, Bolton, during refurbishment of the travel office. *Cyril Golding*

The running-sheet document:

P41 RIBBLE MOTOR SERVICES LTD. FRENCHWOOD, PRESTON.		Date				Ref.	Miles	S.	
		Day		URBAN BONUS		140	0.4	R.S. No. AZ.94	
Driver		Conductor		Reptd.	Mins.	P.	142	60.1	
							570	41.7	Bus Duty 9 & 2.AZ
OFF 2111	S.P. 2	OFF 2116	S.P. 2	Intls.	256				Roster Duty No.
ON 1242	S.A. 57	ON 1236	S.A. 57	Reptd.					
	S.R.		S.R.						
Payable Time 8h. 0u.	L.O.	Payable Time 8h. 1u.	L.O.	Intls.					Wage No.
D.T.	O.M. BONUS					6.4p	Total 102.2		

MILES	BUS No.	U.B. mins.	REF. No.	SERV. No.	DEPART	TIME	DEPART	TIME
					JOURNEYS REF. 570 VIA TORRISHOLME: REF. 142 DIRECT			
					BUS DUTY 9.AZ			
0.4		2	140	140	County Garage	1243		
		15	142	142	Euston Road	1250	* (SEE FOOTNOTE No.1)	
30.4		17			Lancaster	1306	Garstang	1342
			142	142	Gt. Eccleston	1359	* (SEE FOOTNOTE No.2)	
					Blackpool Talbot Rd. (arr) 1419			
		17			do do	1445		
29.7		13			Gt. Eccleston	1505	* (SEE FOOTNOTE No.3)	
					Garstang	1525	* (SEE FOOTNOTE Nos.4 & 5)	
					Lancaster	1600		
					County Garage	1613	Rel. for Morecambe	
					DRIVER & CONDUCTOR OFF DUTY 1615 to 1646			
					BUS DUTY 2.AZ			
			570	570	County Garage	1708	Heysham Towers	1727
10.4		49	570	570	Lancaster	1815	do	1852
13.9		64	570	570	do	1935	do	2012
13.9		64	570	570	do	2055		
3.5		15			County Garage	2110	Rel. for Heysham	

25.9.72. - 120 - JGW/AMM

*No.1 DISPLAY WINDOW STICKERS "FOR PRESTON". THROUGH BOOKINGS ACROSS GARSTANG IN THE PRESTON DIRECTION APPLY ON THIS JOURNEY. SEE FARE TABLE F.367.

*No.2 AT GT. ECCLESTON, WHITE BULL, CONNECT WITH BUS FROM PRESTON DUE 1356. DELAY THREE MINUTES IF NECESSARY.

*No.3 CONNECT AT GT. ECCLESTON WITH PRESTON BUS DEPARTING METHODIST CHURCH AT 1508.

*No.4 ACCEPT THROUGH BOOKINGS ACROSS GARSTANG FROM THE PRESTON DIRECTION IN ACCORDANCE WITH FARE TABLE F.367.

*No.5 ON ARRIVAL AT GARSTANG, CHECK THAT SERVICE 140 HAS ARRIVED FROM PRESTON (DUE AT 22 MINS. PAST THE HOUR) FOR TRANSFER OF PASSENGERS. IF IN DOUBT CALL INTO GARSTANG OFFICE FOR INSTRUCTIONS.

Ribble was famous for its running-sheet system. Every day each crew was issued with a new sheet (from purpose-built filing systems) and submitted it at the end of duty. If a part duty were done the other part would be crossed out in red. The crew filled in their details and the bus fleet number, and, so the argument went, from this one document came all details needed for the payroll (the various differing payments being detailed) — mileages, engineering records and so on. In Ribble parlance a bus was a 'machine'. If a washed one needed to be collected the running sheet announced: 'Obtain clean machine'. So the Beatles worked for Ribble! This sheet is from AZ (Morecambe) and covers some Blackpools, finishing off on the 'track'. Note all the subsidiary information — impressive for a centralised system — and the pay time, broken up into hours and units. One unit equalled six minutes — a bureaucracy-reducing exercise introduced by Bottomley in the early '50s. *Joe Gornall collection*

Making machines do the work. The 37 Willebrew ticket-listing machines in Ticket Audit in 1953 *(top left)*, the same room in 1957 *(bottom left)*, with the Powers Samas punch-card system, and the 1004 ICT computer system, in 1965 *(right)*. Look at the effects on staff numbers. *Roger Davies collection*

Ribble was also a great film-maker. Its first production, *A Day in the Country*, was made by the film unit in 1956 and shown to 13,000 people at more than 50 showings throughout the operating area. It and subsequent yearly offerings were intended to promote travel by Ribble coach, and more than 100,000 people had already seen a Ribble movie by the time *Ireland is for Holidays* hit the screens in 1963; during that January and February this could be viewed with free-admission tickets at 34 venues ranging from Middleton Public Baths to the Co-operative Hall in Baldwin Street, St Helens. The Publicity Department filmed on location using this Kennex-bodied Bedford shooting brake (no pun intended!), KCK 649, complete with fleetname. The whole thing was edited — with music, sound-effects and a commentary — by Ribble's charismatic Publicity Officer, George Bell. George had started as a parcel boy in Lancaster and is generally credited with coining the phrase 'Ribble serves all Britain', as shown on bus 1369 on page 44.
Ribble Enthusiasts' Club

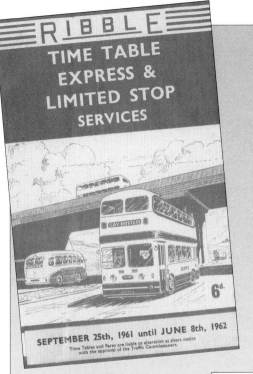

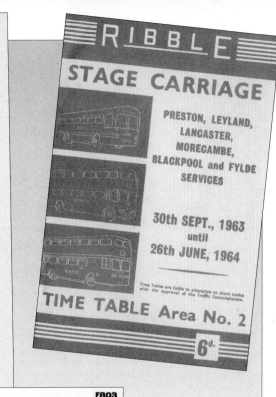

Top left and top right:
Timetables from the early 1960s.
David A. Powell collection

Top centre:
An example of the loose-leaf style of timetable introduced in 1975. Note how each had a number.
Roger Davies collection

Right:
Fare table for use at Liverpool (AW), Aintree (AY) and Wigan (AT). Note this too has a number and an interesting introduction date.
Roger Davies collection

| Services | 317 | ST. HELENS, PRESCOT and LIVERPOOL | | | | | | | | | | F803 |
| | 320 | WIGAN, ABRAM, ASHTON, ST. HELENS, PRESCOT and LIVERPOOL | | | | | | | | | | |

Stage Nos.							SINGLE FARES ONLY				CR20/182 (317)	
											CR20/254 (320)	
12	WIGAN, Market Square (12)●											
13	15	INCE, Oldhall (13)●										
14	15	15	ABRAM, Warrington Road (14)●									
15	20	15	15	STUBSHAW CROSS, Rams Head (15)●								
16	20	20	15	10	ASHTON, Gerrard Street (16)●							
17	25	20	20	15	10	HAYDOCK LODGE, Entrance (17)●						
18	30	25	25	20	15	10	HAYDOCK, Rams Head (18)					
19	30	30	25	25	20	8	BLACKBROOK, Huntsman (19)					
20	30	30	30	25	25	14	8	REDGATE (20)				
21	35	35	30	25	25	20	14	8	ST. HELENS, Victoria Square or Corporation Street (21)			
22	40	40	35	30	30	25	20	14		ECCLESTON, Lane Ends (22)		
23	40	40	35	35	30	25	20	20	8	PRESCOT, Evans Street or Westminster Bank (23)		
24	40	40	40	35	35	30	30	25	25	10	10	HUYTON, Jct. Huyton Lane (24)	
25	45	40	40	35	35	30	30	25	25	15	15	15	HUYTON, Blue Bell Lane (25)
26	45	45	40	40	40	35	35	30	30	25	25	25	20	KNOTTY ASH, Queens Drive (26)
27	50	50	45	45	45	40	40	40	35	30	30	30	25	LIVERPOOL, Adelphi Htl, Brownlow Hill (27)
28	50	50	45	45	45	45	40	40	40	40	35	30	30	LIVERPOOL, Strand/Paradise St. Busway (28)

Local Passengers are not carried point to point in the City of Liverpool.

Children's Fares — Children aged 3 years and above but under 15 years, half adult rates plus fractions of a new penny (except within the Greater Manchester and MPTE Areas — see Tables F700 and F800).
Area—see below).

● **GREATER MANCHESTER COUNCIL AREA**—For Special Conditions applicable to journeys **wholly** confined to the section of route between **Wigan**, Bus Station and **Ashton**, Station or across the Area boundary at **Ashton**, Station—see Table F700.

SPECIAL FARES AND CONDITIONS MERSEYSIDE. P.T.E. AREA (Ashton Station—Liverpool) see Table F800.

MERSEYSIDE P.T.E. TRAVELLER TICKETS ARE NOT VALID ON THESE SERVICES

| Ribble Motor Services Ltd. Fares Sheet | | 29 February 1976 | No. 9352 |
| Depot(s) AW AY AT | | mb. 1000 | Replacing 9163 |

15. The Ribble 'Family'

One of the earliest examples of this remarkable phenomenon again involves Elsie Taylor. In 1923 she left to marry Thomas Hannon, who worked at King Street Saw Mills in Lancaster. In 1934, at the depths of the Depression, when jobs were scarce, he lost his job, and Elsie did no more

than write to Major Hickmott. The result was Thomas's appointment as a temporary cash clerk in Kendal from 28 April (a Saturday), three days after his job offer, on £2 10s (£2.50) a week. He was expected to work at any of the Company's offices. Thomas became a much-respected member of the Kendal team and an active trade-union official, being appointed Chief Clerk on 8 November 1952 (at £8 per week) and retiring almost exactly eight years later, after more than 25 years' service.

The same spirit was still evident in 1971. William Leese, then General Manager, had been taken ill and on his return to work wrote in the *Bulletin*, saying how grateful he and his wife were for 'the many messages of sympathy and goodwill we received from members of the Ribble Family'.

Barbara Robinson's father worked in Ulverston depot and never thought about any other job. Her husband joined him, and New Year parties at home were made up of Ribble people. They even provided lodgings for some of the staff.

Major Hickmott's reply to Elsie Taylor's approach of 1934 — look at the list of offices now! The letter gives an insight into the Major's character and compares favourably with todays methods. *courtesy Kathleen Morris*

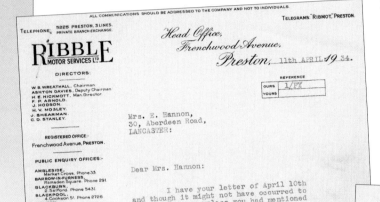

Kendal depot had its own cartoonist, and the event depicted actually occurred at Sandilands terminus when Thomas Hannon was so concerned about passengers' safety on ice that he slipped over himself! Royal Tiger 393 was at Kendal from October 1958 until January 1959, so the incident can be dated pretty accurately. An excellent example of the 'Family' at work! *courtesy Kathleen Morris*

Annual Visit to Headquarters

MORE than 40 members of the Ribble Enthusiasts' Club visited Head Office and the Frenchwood Works on December 1st for the 8th Annual General Meeting of the Club.

On arrival at Headquarters they were welcomed by their president, Mr. George Brook, our General Manager.

Prior to holding their annual meeting, the enthusiasts toured the Frenchwood Works where they saw vehicles under repair and examined the new Body Finishing and Paint Shops.

A visit was also made to Publicity Department where the members listened to experts explaining the intricacies of bus time-table compilation and saw posters being produced by the silk-screen method.

Members were then entertained to lunch and during the proceedings Mr. W. G. Hunniball, Assistant to the General Manager, extended the good wishes of Ribble and its people to the Club. Then for one whole hour there was a barrage of questions.

The members adjourned to the board-room where during the afternoon they held their annual meeting, exchanged photographs of buses old and new and made plans for the future.

The 1963 programme will include a visit to Cardiff.

Spoilt for choice ! To help make up their minds about their next coach tour members of the Ribble Enthusiasts' Club, along with their President, Mr. George Brook, General Manager, examine a destination blind. Mr. Brook is the seventh standing on the left. On Mr. Brook's left is David Verity, one of our traffic apprentices and Clive Turner another of our traffic apprentices is the twelfth standing from the left. Mr. T. B. Collinge, the Records Officer and founder member of the Club is standing to the right of the blind and behind him is Mr. P. Brooks, the Club's Secretary.

Don't say we didn't tell you

Open all your doors at midnight on Christmas Eve and the evil spirits will take themselves off and not return.

* * *

Be careful not to hang your holly before you have hung your mistletoe, or evil spirits may come down the chimney.

* * *

If you eat twelve mince pies on Christmas day you may get good luck in all the twelve months of the coming year (on the other hand you might well get indigestion.)

* * *

Mistletoe can be full of peril as some of you know ! But for luck's sake start off by kissing someone whose colouring is opposite to that of your own. This applies only to the first kiss ; after that, fair-haired boy can kiss fair-haired girl without courting any repercussions — other than the ones you know about already !

* * *

Don't forget to count the berries on the mistletoe. An old legend gives you the right to claim a kiss for each one.

* * *

According to an old Welsh legend, a decapitated shadow on Christmas Day means you'll be a "gonner" by the next. So don't get into a position where your shadow is headless.

The Ribble Enthusiasts' Club was formed on 19 May 1954 by the late Tom Collinge, a man with an encyclopædic knowledge of the Company. Within a year Ribble had recognised the professionalism of the club, and the latter's first AGM was held at Frenchwood. This became a regular event until 1990, with members meeting senior officers, seeing behind the scenes and taking lunch. Coach tours were started in 1960, one of the earliest, in September of that year, being undertaken in a 'Gay Hostess'. A regular bulletin is produced, and the fact that the club is still active — indeed, celebrating 50 years in 2004 — in its aim of bringing together people who like to know everything about Ribble gives some indication of the Company's allure. (Membership details can be found on page 112.) It was a mutual respect, the marriage in 1959 of Tom Collinge and Miss A. E. Wilson being reported in the Ribble *Bulletin*; whilst it was unusual to report a wedding not involving staff, the *Bulletin* 'makes no excuse', even including a picture of the newly-weds on their 'red carpet' — the destination blind from Cheetah 1582! This picture shows the 1962 AGM, attended by George Brook. And just savour the christmas legends. *Roger Davies collection*

'Whilst I was growing up, ours was a Ribble house,' she recalls. No doubt some were involved in the practice of taking a Royal Tiger damson-picking in the Lyth Valley! Edmund Chambers was a running-shift fitter at Penrith. 'Each depot was a family,' he remembers; 'they were the best years of my life.' A former NBC trainee at the Company, Paul Hill, remembers his return as Area Superintendent (Northern). 'It was like coming back into the bosom of the family; people made it clear I was welcome back.' John Slater moved into Frenchwood from a driving job in 1973 and recalls that 'the senior management treated their staff, including the new recruit, with courtesy and consideration, fostering the view that we were all part of the Ribble family'.

Mike Shires points out that 25% of staff had relatives or family working for the Company, and 25% had over 25 years' service by the early '60s. This also reflected in the way Ribble treated its staff. Bruce Maund recalls a depot superintendent who, having suffered badly as a result of running a busy large depot bedevilled by enemy action during the war, was given a quiet 12-bus rural depot with no loss of pay. Jobs were found at Frenchwood for other staff past their sell-by date — one in

particular, remembers Bruce, who used to doze off and emit alarming snores 'which made the uninitiated think he was suffering some medical emergency'. When Ribble's mighty bureaucracy discovered that it had failed to detect some staff achieving retirement age, they were allowed to stay on for several months.

This attitude affected customers. Vic Clarke grew up near Renwick, in the Eden Valley, and, having passed his Eleven Plus — 'think they got the papers mixed up' — had to travel into Penrith for the Grammar School. Throughout his time there the crews were the same, based at a dormy shed at Kirkoswald ('KO' to all but Ribble, to which it was 'BN') sited in Lace's garage and opened in 1932. Conductors Pickering, McVittie, Graham and Bell (who checked every ticket because he wanted to be an inspector) helped Drivers Bowers, Hardy, Renvoice and Johnston (whose gear-changes were a bit rough, as he'd been a tank driver), and all are well remembered by Vic. John Hurst recalls colourful characters like the conductress on the Penrith–Carlisle run who would shout out in the Cumbrian dialect: 'All them for Plumpton, lowp out!' Rosemary McKinlay remembers Ribble buses as 'just there, always on time whatever the weather or conditions'. Audrey Mathews can bear this out. On one wild snowy night she conducted a bus from Carlisle to Sebergham, getting a bit lost going and very lost returning. Finally the driver bade her struggle through the blizzard to a remote farmhouse to ask directions. The farmer's wife was confident: 'Easy —walk to the left, wait at the crossroads and there'll be a Ribble bus along in 10 minutes.' Ted Gahan regularly drove Aintree route 201, a two-hourly, one-bus affair through the village of Melling, wherein resided Beatrice. This lady, aware there was little rest time in the shift and despite being disabled, would wait at her gate with tea and homemade cakes for the crew! Mike Lockyer, working at Skipton, the only depot 'int' enemy territory' (Yorkshire), remembers driving 'Embsays', where the driver was regarded as more of a neighbour and friend; 'It was the norm for someone to pop out and ask the driver to fetch a white loaf, paper or prescription, my oddest task being to bring a coil of barbed wire for a farmer from Manby's the Ironmonger.'

But it was in the social side that the 'family' really made itself known. From small beginnings a vast Sports Committee grew up, organising fixtures in sports and pastimes varying from football to crib and from snooker to dominoes throughout the Company. Such was the scale of it, having 900 registered members, that it

◄ The 693 service, originally to Cardurnock, was cut back to Bowness-on-Solway (CC in Ribblespeak), where the one-bus dormy shed attached to Carlisle was to be found on Main Street. Originally run by just about the Company's only non-Leyland purchases of the 1930s (seven Dennis Aces), owing to a weight restriction it later became home to the Sentinels, one (281) expiring in flames in the town. By this September 1980 view 313 — the only one of the 49 Marshall-bodied RESLs to stray as far north as Carlisle — had become CC's regular bus. Flooding on this low-lying marshland on the estuary of the Rivers Esk and Eden was a monthly occurrence, but somehow the CC boys always seemed to get through. *Barrie Wright*

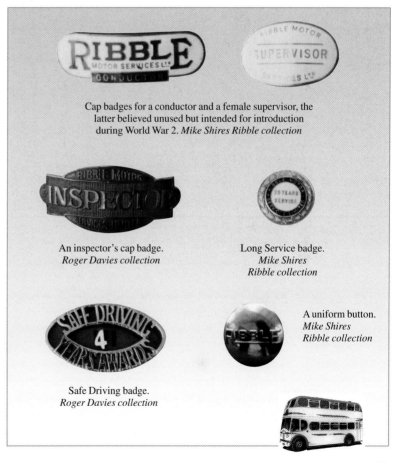

Cap badges for a conductor and a female supervisor, the latter believed unused but intended for introduction during World War 2. *Mike Shires Ribble collection*

An inspector's cap badge. *Roger Davies collection*

Long Service badge. *Mike Shires Ribble collection*

Safe Driving badge. *Roger Davies collection*

A uniform button. *Mike Shires Ribble collection*

was split into North and South, with a titanic final fixture between the two. This took place at the Leyland Motors sports ground in Chorley. Sports presentation evenings were famous, as was the Annual Ball. This remarkable event included the crowning of the 'Miss Ribble' beauty queen. Taking over the whole of the Winter Gardens, in the 1930s this was, according to Press reports, 'one of Blackpool's biggest and most impressive social functions', with 5,000 guests, six mayors and the most famous dance bands of the day. It continued; Dave Kershaw recalls that in the 1960s entertainment was provided by not only the 'Hollies' but also the 'Yardbirds', when both were at the height of their fame. Throughout the patch children's Christmas parties and outings were arranged. Liz Wilson remembers her father paying a little a week from his wages, then all the children setting off in a convoy of Ribble 'deckers to see the Pantomime on Ice in Manchester: 'We found it very exciting — it wasn't often in those days that we went on trips without our parents. Happy Days!'

It wasn't only just pleasure. Important business matters were also dealt with at social events, long-service and safe-driving awards being presented by the Chairman at grand functions in the Spanish Room of the Blackpool Tower complex. In 1957 no fewer than 2,237 safe-driving awards were presented. The 'family' enjoyed a good get-together.

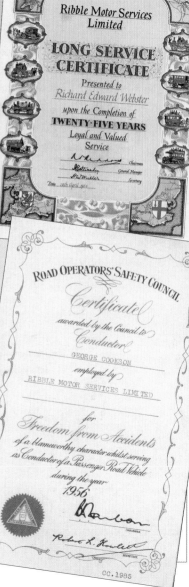

Above:
Some formal presentations took place locally; this one, held in Kendal Town Hall, was presumably a Northern Area function. *Christina Lowther*

Top right:
Long Service certificate of 1954.
Ribble Vehicle Preservation Trust

Lower right:
Road Safety awards 1956/7.
Ribble Enthusiasts' Club

RIBBLE
MOTOR SERVICES LTD.

—AND—
SUBSIDIARY
COMPANIES

ALSO
ASSOCIATED
COMPANIES

41/55 S. 10m. 19/3/35.

FROM STAGE COACH
TO
STATE COACH
AND THE
"RIBBLE" STAFF BALL

WINTER GARDENS, BLACKPOOL,
WEDNESDAY, MARCH 27TH, 1935.

Beauty Queen Finalists . . . . . Travel Programme

CARLISLE (Carlisle Queen) Dep. 1.28 p.m.
(Penrith Queen) Dep. 9.4 a.m.

WINDERMERE
(Ulverston Queen)
Dep. 2.18 p.m.

KENDAL (Kendal Queen) Dep. 2.30 p.m.

MORECAMBE
(Lancaster Queen)
Dep. 3.6 p.m.

LANCASTER (Lancaster Queen) Dep.3.30 p.m.

SKIPTON
(Skipton
Queen)
Dep. 1.30 p.m.

THORNTON   LITTLE THORNTON
(Blackpool Queen) (Fleetwood Queen)

ELSWICK (Garstang Queen)
Dep. 3.3 p.m.

WHALLEY (Clitheroe Queen)
Dep. 2.50 p.m.

BURNLEY (Burnley Queen)
Dep. 2.40 p.m.

BLACKPOOL
Arr. 6.15 p.m.
(Approx)

TO BLACKPOOL & RIBBLE STAFF BALL

ARRIVE
PRESTON
(Approx)

ASHTON
(Preston Queen)
Dep. 3.45 p.m.

BLACKBURN
(Blackburn Queen)
Dep. 3.30 p.m.

ABBEY VILLAGE (Chorley Queen)
Dep. 3.15 p.m.

CHORLEY Dep. 3.46 p.m.

Queens
depart for Blackpool
at 5.30 p.m.
(approx)

WATERLOO (Liverpool Queen)
Dep. 1.45 p.m.

WIGAN
(Wigan Queen)
Dep. 3.2 p.m.

BOLTON (Bolton
Queen)
Dep. 3.17

MANCH

LIVERPOOL (Liverpool Queen)
Dep. 2.20 p.m.

MISS ANNA LEE OF GAUMONT-B
FILM FA
THE BEAUTY QUEE

The Queens *shall* go to the Ball.
The 1935 pick-ups; note the precise
timings — and an early 'stagecoach'
reference! *Mike Shires Ribble collection*

Invitations, tickets (including one for
the Coronation Ball of 1937) and a
programme for the 1936 Ball.
Mike Shires Ribble collection

GRAND
ANNUAL BALL

WINTER GARDENS
BLACKPOOL

WEDNESDAY, MARCH 25th,
1936

PROGRAMME

RIBBLE
AND W. C. STANDERWICK, LTD.

GRAND   4376
CORONATION
BALL

EMPRESS BALLROOM
WINTER GARDENS
BLACKPOOL

WEDNESDAY, APRIL 14th.

DANCING TO
NORMAN NEWMAN
and The Tower Band
5 p.m. – 2 a.m.

Ticket

RIBBLE
MOTOR SERVICES LTD.   0000

ANNUAL BALL

EMPRESS BALLROOM :: WINTER GARDENS
BLACKPOOL
WEDNESDAY, MARCH 29th, 1939

The 1968 Ball; mini-dresses on mini-bikes
in the mini-race. *Roger Davies collection*

Steward's badge.
*Mike Shires
Ribble collection*

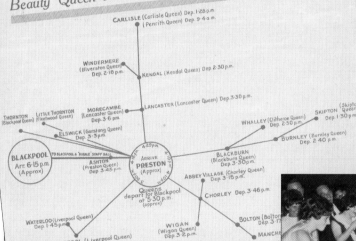

Part Three: The Fall of Ribble

16. Bananas

As the '60s wore on George Brook's comments in the *Bulletin* became littered with tales of woe. In 1966 the compulsory introduction of a sick-pay scheme, a 40-hour week without loss of pay and extra National Insurance payments to cover Redundancy Payments Act requirements cost Ribble an additional £295,000, while Government taxation continued to cause problems; this was without a wage increase, and labour costs per mile were now 5.6 times what they had been in 1939. The year's new-vehicle intake of 106 vehicles —

a twelfth of the fleet — was costing £600,000. The 1966 fares increase aimed to bring in £220,000 and, due to the cumbersome procedure, took about three months to get authorised. Readers can do the sums for themselves. On top of all this, the Government was wittering about 'Conurbation Transport Authorities' and holding meetings in Ribble's patch to discuss them. It is heartening to see Mr Brook spending just as much time emphasising the teamwork necessary to keep the Company successful.

What's the full story about 1928's Furness Omnibus Co?

JOHN Hambler, chairman of the Barrow Transport Group had this grand photo of the short-lived but enthusiastic Furness Omnibus Co Ltd staff in 1928 passed to him in a town club recently.

It will be added to the already large portfolio of history capturing photos held by the group which include gems of the Michaelson Road bridge looking as busy as Westminster Bridge as thousands of men and a sea of buses move homeward at the end of the Vickers day.

The Furness Omnibus Company only had a short life, from being founded in 1928 to being taken over by Ribble in 1930.

Its garage used to be in Station Road, Dalton, on a site now occupied by Terry Chemicals.

BTG member Phil Cousins thinks the company was made up of owner-drivers and wonders if some of the younger staff at the front of the picture might be sons of the owners.

The fine old snub-nosed buses are thought to be Leyland Lionesses.

The staff certainly look a business-like bunch, with some of them more cheerful than others. Presumably Ribble made them an offer they couldn't turn down.

The transport group would love to hear from anyone who knows more about this short-lived company or who could yield important memorabilia such as timetables and badges, or stories from the days of operation.

Phil Cousins can be contacted on Barrow 837933.

Ribble was responsible for some little-known but delightful parts of the UK. One such was the Furness Peninsula, this coming into Ribble territory with the purchase in 1930, for £45,000, of the Furness Omnibus Co. This was run originally from the latter's depot in Dalton (closed in 1968) and then from Ribble's 'own' in Ulverston. Dalton was notable in that it consisted of separate sheds, each with a bus running number — prefixed by the depot code (BT) — painted on the door, so that drivers would know which bus to take. This view, with the Lakeland fells as a backdrop, epitomises the scenery on the rural route between Ulverston and Barrow (which Corporation shared the main-road route through Dalton) via Beckside and Leese (no connection with the General Manager). Some journeys missed out Scales, these being 527s instead of 526s, as demonstrated by PD2 1436 at Roose in August 1970. *Eckersley / Photobus*

The enthusiastic staff of the short-lived Furness Omnibus Co, pictured in 1928. *Marjorie Lindsay*

One of the most successful routes in the Lake District is that between Ambleside and Dungeon Ghyll, at the head of Langdale. Quite apart from serving one of the most splendid of destinations, it attracts year-round support from walkers and climbers. A well-laden (and absolutely immaculate) 'Little Leopard', 680 of 1966, is pictured at Dungeon Ghyll in May 1970. *Eckersley / Photobus*

Ribble buses served most of the literary parts of the Lake District, passing both Wordsworth's house and the site of his ''ost of gorlden daffodils'. (Well, he *was* from the North.) No 681 here is on a more off-the-wall sort of literary mission, passing along Kentmere, the inspiration for 'Postman Pat'. This was deeply rural and didn't survive for long after this February 1970 photograph was taken. You realise what a sensational job Northern Area engineers did in keeping the buses so smart when traffic people made them do this kind of thing. *Eckersley / Photobus*

Continuing our literary theme, another of the 'Little Leopards' so associated with the Lakes, this time Ambleside's 662, passes through Near Sawrey on the infrequent service from Ferry Landing, on Windermere. This was home to Beatrix Potter, and the Tower Bank Arms, visible behind 662 (and to be recommended!), features in her books. This view was recorded in June 1970. *Eckersley / Photobus*

This captures the essence of the 555 route at Troutbeck Bridge in March 1970. Heading to Lancaster from Keswick is 1961, a Northern Counties-bodied Atlantean PDR1/2. Margaret Dixon, whose parents had lodged Ribble crews, boarded a 555 in 1950, taking the last available seat which was next to a young man. He offered her a cheese sandwich — she declined — and on leaving the bus in Lancaster, asked her out to the pictures. They have been married for 54 years. *Eckersley / Photobus*

RIBBLE
Staff
BULLETIN

NUMBER 207
AUGUST, 1967

On 19 August 1967 a very interesting experiment was started in Formby, where a new network of town services was introduced on the flat-fare principle, passengers paying the exact fare into a Setright machine, allowing OMO working; cleverly the machine quoted the adult fare in figures and the child's using pictures. Year-old Leopard 640 had its already limited capacity reduced to 36 and adopted DP livery and the lower-case style of fleetname that was to become standard a year later. It later moved on to Penrith, retaining these colours for a while. *Roger Davies collection*

EXAMINATIONS AND TRAINING

EXAMINATION results—when will they be published and what will they be?—have been well in the minds of a great many young people, and some not so young, during the past few weeks.

The first results of the examinations taken in 1967 by our trainees, apprentices and others who have been studying to better themselves are announced in this issue of the *Staff Bulletin* and others which have still to be published will be included in next month's issue.

I take this opportunity sincerely to congratulate all the successful candidates and express [...] hope that they will continue with their studies and work for so long as it is necessary to enable th[...] to qualify in their chosen careers.

I commiserate with those who have not passed and hope that in trying again they will succe[...]

Never has the need for well educated, well trained and capable staff been greater than it is to[...] Never have the opportunities for young people to gain knowledge and experience and to be pr[...] trained been greater than they are to-day.

The many technical and commercial colleges and colleges of further education in the Co[...] area have published their programmes for the coming session and enrolment for the greatest [...] of courses ever offered in the history of education and training in this country will be taki[...] during the next few days.

I want you all to know—and I particularly say this to the newcomers to our business[...] Company has always been anxious and now, more than ever, is it keen to foster the pursuit o[...] in the subjects and techniques appropriate to our business and is ready to help with the c[...] books and tuition and examination fees.

Departmental heads and depot officials can answer enquiries and expert advice is [...] the asking from the Company's Training Officer.

"Flat-fare" Service for Formby

The Setright Multi Set coin-operated tickets machine is sited just behind the driver. Better circulation space near to the machine has resulted from reducing the number of seats from 44 to 36. On the bulkhead above the ticket machine is a route map of the three services in diagramatic form. In addition to the parcel racks, there is parcel accommodation alongside and behind the ticket machine and in a bay on the nearside opposite.

2

FROM Saturday, August 19th the Company has been operating a local circular service in Formby with a "flat fare"—passengers pay 6d. (3d. for children) no matter how far they travel, and they obtain their own tickets from a coin-operated machine.

Operating six days a week from Monday to Saturday, the service is operated in three parts, each forming a circle but running continuously.

The special bus being used for this service is a single decker 30ft. 6in. and 8ft. 2½in. wide based on a Leyland Leopard chassis. It has 36 seats instead of the normal 44 in one-man buses.

The fewer seats have enabled space to be provided for the installation of the self-service ticket machine.

THE FRONT PAGE PHOTOGRAPH

THIS is the bus that is operating on the Formby circular services—see this page. It differs from our other buses in that its livery is predominantly cream instead of red, and with a newly-styled fleet name it is easily distinguishable from our other service buses.

Passengers enter the bus at the front nearside and insert their money (6d. for an adult and 3d. in the case of children) in the ticket machine situated just behind the driver's compartment on the offside.

The coin-operated ticket machine is only in its trial stages and so the driver is also able to issue tickets.

During the two weeks prior to its introduction the service and the vehicle received much Press publicity locally which undoubtedly helped the reasonably smooth operation which so far has been experienced.

The standard Setright machine instructions have been amplified by the addition of a special clear plastics-covered board, incorporated to help children quickly understand are three 1d. coins and 3d. piece.

It would be easy to imagine that Ribble only turned to Bristol because of NBC, but the age of the buses undermines that, the first 10 REs being delivered just three months after the sale of BET's bus interests and seven months before NBC was formed; even the second batch of 30 arrived in time (in 1969) to be given traditional Ribble livery and fleetnames. Much more likely was Ribble's desire for a rear-engined single-deck and its disillusionment with Leyland's offering, the Panther, one of which came in 1964. Here ECW-bodied RELL6G 253 of the 1969 delivery reverses off Preston's astonishing bus station on a local service when both were pretty new. Passenger access to the island loading platforms was by means of subways that became treacherous in the wet and host to undesirables at night. Drivers, meanwhile, were aware that no one should be walking across the apron and acted accordingly. Do planners live in the real world? *Peter Yates collection*

Liz Wilson's father, Eric Ganner, was a driver at Preston. Even on late shifts he would be up early to make sure he looked the part — pressed trousers, clean shirt and shining shoes. He did a lot of work as secretary of the TGWU at the depot and prepared for meetings in his own time. 'It wasn't done grudgingly,' she says; 'they simply wanted passengers to enjoy travelling by Ribble.' During school holidays her mother would take Eric to work so that she could use the car to take the children to the beach. They would have to return to Selbourne Street depot at about midnight, and Eric would take her through the bus wash in his bus before handing it over to the cleaners. 'Obviously worked,' remembers Liz; 'Ribble buses were always clean.' Note taking the car; these folks probably had some concession from Ribble. It shows just how quickly the car had established itself in life — a fact not lost on successive postwar governments, which continued to rack up fuel tax. The fact that this applied to buses as well means that politicians were as much to blame for the industry's decline as were cars and television. They must have

been dark days indeed, compared with the Swingin' scene (born in Ribble Land) and the confident, professional exterior on show.

The fateful lunch on 8 May 1967 between Transport Minister Barbara Castle, BET Chairman Spencer Wills and Reggie Wilson, Chairman of the Transport Holding Co, resulted in the sale of BET's bus interests to the THC. It caused some gloom at first but strangely helped remove the threat of conurbation transport authorities, as the THC wouldn't have wanted a decimated BET. Unions simply wanted a State-owned BET. Thus Ribble and its three subsidiaries became State-owned for the first time on 13 February 1968. On 1 January 1969 they became part of the National Bus Company, bringing with them 1,205 buses, 5,169 staff, 26 depots, 11 dormy sheds, 38 travel offices and 141,984,719 passengers carried 51,166,014 miles over 5,654 route miles. During 1970 it made its first-ever loss. Ribble was not alone; birds were coming home to roost throughout the bus industry. It was 'no wheels on my wagon' time. The BET Chairman must have allowed himself a wry smile.

Curiously the first Bristol double-deckers repeated the single-deckers' trick, arriving just in time to receive traditional livery, albeit with lower-case names. Here NBC influence is much more likely. They were whipped off to convert Carlisle city services to OMO, with a farebox system which restricted them to such work from 3 June 1972. This was unfortunate, as Carlisle had been the pioneer of highbridge working, and the low height of these buses was unnecessary. At least 1971-built 1979 (one of only two with 'J' registrations) had time to take the Fylde Coast air, being seen here in Cleveleys *en route* to Blackpool — an early example of an OMO double-decker. Ribble had had a terrible 1970, and good progress was made the following year in expanding this form of operation. *Peter Yates collection*

It all goes a bit mad here. In 1970/1, after many years of specifying maximum length and capacity for its coaches, Ribble took 25 shorter (10m) Leopard coaches with 36 well-spaced seats intended for touring work and a further 11 with 43 seats for express work. It doesn't make a great deal of sense, and within six months 1103, along with 1102/4, had been withdrawn and transferred to Standerwick (117-9). You can't help feeling that the plot was being lost, and these machines were somewhat unwanted — sad, because they were pretty little things. No 1103 is seen in Wigan early in its Standerwick career, working a London–Keswick. In the background is a very fine Northern Counties-bodied Titan of Wigan Corporation. *David A. Powell*

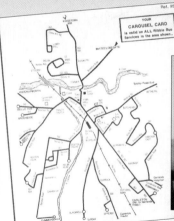

Five days into NBC ownership the local Carlisle services of United were transferred to Ribble, giving it all the city services. This 1977 window-bill shows the full network, with its own ticket. *Roger Davies collection*

Ribble also gained United's out-of-town services including the 686, running to the most northerly outpost of Noblestown, Letter Box Crossroads; this was a super description, for that's all there was, as Leopard 503 demonstrates in August 1976! Negotiations also began for the takeover of services run by Western SMT, which had a depot next to the bus station, and some of whose routes didn't even enter Scotland. *Roger Davies*

17. Ribble's NBC and New Ribble

It's tempting to leave it there, but that would be unfair. It would also be unfair to blame NBC for the 'dreadful' year of 1970. Ribble was 230 drivers, 220 conductors and 55 fitters short, and spare-parts delivery was a nightmare. William Leese met the *Lancashire Evening Post* in an open interview to keep passengers in the picture. The article, headed 'Why we are Under Attack — by Bus Boss', was reproduced in full in the *Bulletin*. Arguably NBC dealt well — better than most — with the horrendous problems facing the industry during the 1970s. Just when it needed friends most, the industry plunged into an orgy of slaughtering fondly held images and inventing others that lost contact, sympathy and understanding. It was a terrible time. Although NBC, after three years of anonymity, finally succumbed to the dead hand of corporate identity, it did retain most of the companies and their names. Ribble survived and, indeed, retained its powerful image. John Underhill, NBC's Insurance Manager, remembers it as 'one of the most loss-prevention-conscious companies in the Group, having a good Health & Safety philosophy and an excellent works accident-prevention booklet. This reflected the attitude of the Central Workshop and good leadership from above.' All NBC companies were equal, some more so than others. Ribble was one — if not *the* one — of those. I longed to work there. And, bless 'em, they sent me there.

When I moved to Kendal I transferred my bank account. Demonstrating the regard in which the Company was held, the bank manager said: 'Don't worry if you go a bit overdrawn at the end of the month; you work for Ribble — we know the money will be in.'

Do you have a colour shot of a white coach? This requires some lateral thinking. This type of Duple Dominant-bodied Leyland Leopard, in white, was Ribble's choice of coach for the best part of a decade, but let's try and spice it up a bit. This wasn't actually a Ribble coach; it belonged to National Travel West, had North Western fleetnames — that's not really the North Western with the Loline on page 44 (although that was the basis of it), nor the one which later took over Ribble's Merseyside operations — and was cared for at Ribble's Hulme Hall Road depot in Manchester. Got it? (Ribble took it all over again in 1984, but that's not the point of the story.) Express coaches worked hard, and this is a terrific example. A typical working for 130 here and its four tachograph-fitted sisters was to leave Manchester for London at 17.00 on a Thursday, and the next day it would do the London–Galway via the Liverpool–Dublin ferry (an Irish crew taking over for the leg in the Republic); then on Sunday it would head back to London, finally returning from there to reach Manchester at around teatime on Tuesday. Ribble's engineers were pretty relaxed about it, so why worry? *David A. Powell*

If you're going to do a job, do it properly. The NBC Corporate Identity freaks set out their stall, and Ribble obliged. Here sister ships 1513 and 1515 stand in Lord Street bus station Southport in 1974, showing the application of the new and former liveries. Even the 'RIBBLE' has been scrubbed off the radiator of 1515, being replaced by a transfer — how petty can you get? It's even got poppy-red windscreen wipers! The purchase of the old Cheshire Lines Committee railway station in 1953, heralded in the *Bulletin* as 'Ribble buys a railway station', led to one of the architects' more interesting projects, the building opening as a bus station on 25 June 1954. Whether it ever justified its £72,500 price tag is doubtful, although it did subsequently house buses, easing the burden on other depots.
David A. Powell

When the old North Western company lost most of its bus services to SELNEC PTE it became a coach-only company and cascaded to other fleets some vehicles that weren't really suitable. In 1973 Ribble got five of these Alexander Y-type-bodied Leopards of a type which, although commonplace elsewhere, was new to the Company. They worked from Manchester, and the X12 thence to Bradford was a regular haunt. Outwardly the same, each had its own character; David Wayman, in his book *Weekend Bus Driver*, advises that our subject here, 1068, was known as 'The Rattler', owing to an affectation that caused its blind (an old North Western one) to slip, turning Manchester into Lowestoft in less than eight miles. It's not looking too bad here, in Halifax in 1977. The other four were named 'The Screamer' (1067), 'The Flyer' (1069), 'The Boneshaker' (1070) and 'The Sewing Machine' (1071). If you need to know why, buy David's book!
David A. Powell

The final design of Ribble AN68 had ECW highbridge bodywork — maybe not the stunner that the Park Royal was, but pretty nice; 29 Bristol VRTs were bodied similarly. No 1507, one of the very last, dating from 1981, is adorned with both NBC 'double N' and Merseyside 'magic whirling wheel' symbols, to demonstrate 'unity of purpose'... or just to indicate that a PTE, whatever that is, exists. It's seen in Lord Street, Liverpool, in July 1981, being followed by a Crosville VRT showing the green version of NBC livery and the height difference between 14ft 6in and 13ft 8in types of ECW body. *Ted Gahan*

As NBC grappled with the problems there was a high turnover of senior staff. George Brook had left to move on up the NBC ladder, being replaced by W. Leese, who, on retirement in 1972, was replaced by W. Hunniball, who, on retirement in 1974, was replaced by Irwin Dalton. In 1973 Robert Brook became Regional Director (Western Region), covering Ribble, and in 1977 Fred Dark became General Manager. All three moved on to very senior positions in NBC, Brook and Dalton ending up as Chairman and Chief Executive. Clearly, Ribble did them no harm, but whether this changing-about helped Ribble is another matter. Certainly all these very able folk kept alive the Company spirit; Irwin Dalton, for example, reintroduced the invitation of long-serving staff to Frenchwood. The Ribble 'family' still thrived at depot level, and there remained great pride in the firm, but it wasn't the same.

An early casualty was the *Bulletin*, swept away by NBC's tabloid *Bus* in 1972. That year saw the first lady driver, Mrs Margaret Joyce Peter from Blackburn, to be followed in 1977 by Mrs Sylvia Kendall of Preston, the first lady inspector. Driver E. Atkinson of Carlisle achieved 40 years' accident-free driving in 1972, and in 1977 William Catterall of Frenchwood and John Nuttall of Burnley became Ribble's first 50-year men. Staff were also being honoured; for example, Inspector George Scattergood of Kendal received the BEM in 1975, and long-serving Frenchwood Works Manager Ron Hopkins the MBE in 1976.

Withdrawal of the 1959 Atlanteans began in 1971 after the normal full life of 12 years. However, the dire shortage of double-deckers caused by lengthy delays in the delivery of new ones extended many lives, and 1616 here lasted until 1977 (which just goes to show what you can do when you have to). Accordingly it gained NBC livery, being seen so adorned outside Garstang depot. This depot stopped maintaining its own buses in 1963, three 'deckers being supplied thereafter from Preston for the Preston–Garstang route, two from Blackpool for the Blackpool–Garstang routes, two from Morecambe for the Morecambe–Burnley route and two single-deckers from Lancaster for Garstang local OMO routes. *Dave Cousins*

Grange-over-Sands (BV) depot was taken over in two stages from the delightfully named Grange Motor & Cycle Co — buses in 1951, coaches in 1958. It was unusual in that coach drivers were allocated their own coaches, resulting in care being lavished on them. It didn't do to fall out with the engineer though, or such things as a week's supply of oil might get accidentally credited to your machine! Next to the town-centre travel office was a traditional coach stand, where two types of Panorama — Leopards 745 and 780 — are seen touting for business in October 1975. *Roger Davies*

In 1975 the local staff at Penrith had identified that by using spare time and odd short workings they could run a comprehensive town service on an hourly basis at virtually no extra cost. The 646 soon became part of the town's life, often being used as a child-minding service while Mum got in some quality shopping. It showed that even a very centralised outfit could be flexible to local needs, and it was much visited and emulated. 'Little Leopard' 646, featured on this launch leaflet, was actually a Carlisle machine. Oh, by the way, the fare was 6p adult, 4p child. *Roger Davies collection*

The result of Engineering Road Inspector Arthur Marston's efforts in the immediate postwar period: having just crossed Dunmail Raise on Kendal–Keswick route 555, gorgeous Park Royal Atlantean 1384, one of three based at Ambleside, pauses at Grasmere in May 1976. *Roger Davies*

Ribble was involved for a considerable time in planning the replacement bus service for the Alston–Haltwhistle railway, but at the final knockings the local authorities got squeamish and put it out to tender, Ribble losing. Apart from being bad form, this meant that Ribble's long-serving member of staff at Alston dormy shed would have been out of a job. The Ribble 'family' swung into action and were successful in appealing the decision and keeping the man's job — not bad from a large organisation that could easily have said 'Tough!'. The route was good too; freed of the need to visit the closed railway stations (some pretty inaccessible), it provided a much better public service. 'Little Leopard' 676, working the 681, approaches Alston, England's highest market town, in February 1977. *Roger Davies*

A terrific study of Lancashire mill-town scenery past its Glory Days. So is the Ribble bus, a National (443), in Burnley in August 1979 — just look at that pathetic destination blind. *S. J. Butler*

Pendle Hill dominates this Ribble bus as it climbs out of Burnley on a 236 to Bolton in August 1981. The Corporate Identity Thought Police had by now decreed that all-over red should replace the white-stripe livery, and staff countrywide were all busy unpicking that feature from their NBC ties. Although Ribble amassed billions of Nationals, incredibly this is the same one (443) as that shown in the previous picture. Oh, all right, billions equals about 304. *David Wayman*

FAREWELL TO CONDUCTORS

The 26th Day of September is a date we won't forget,
For that's the day that Ribble drop their biggest clanger yet;
Conductors jobs are finished, no argument or fuss;
and one-man-operation is the way to run a bus.

They offered OMO training to decker drivers and their mates,
They promised brand new buses and attractive OMO rates;
"Cardinal" Quinn won't try it, he knows he couldn't cope,
besides, he's busy planning next year's visit by the pope.

Our Senior man George Wilson is retiring full of smiles,
and now our Senior driver is that great man Dennis Isles;
Jack Adams too is leaving, he's achieved his greatest wish,
to see the last of Ribble and have some time to fish.

There's little Derrick Phoenix who doesn't want to go,
He's been here nearly 30 years and leaving is a blow;
He's the last of the famous vikings, but OMO's not his style,
so he's taking his redundancy and trying hard to smile.

On the other hand there's "Clogger" Clegg, who's broken every rule,
No Ribble boss can tame him, he's as stubborn as a mule;
They've tried to sack him many times but "Clogger" doesn't care
He'll happily go down the road with 2 fingers in the air.

We're also going to see the end of Ganner's laughing face,
Always full of jokes and yarns, who can take his place ?
with his knowledge and his humour, he's kept the job alive,
but he should have left us years ago, when he was 65.

As you struggle on a 104, and you're almost in despair,
It's no use checking your offside mirror, for Towers won't be there;
The old "Lead Swinger" is leaving, no more we'll see his face,
but there's plenty more like him all set to take his place.

And so goodbye to all the mates we've known throughout the years
Most of them can't wait to leave and won't shed any ~~tears~~; TEARS.
The job's not what it used to be, and it isn't going to mend,
If you try to understand it, it will drive you round the bend.

▲ At 23.06 on 29 January 1982 the last Ribble bus worked by a
conductor left Chorley for Blackburn on service 259. But it was
on 25 September 1981 that the last buses that could *only* be worked
with a conductor had made their final journeys, three at Preston and
four at Morecambe. One of the latter, 1850, numerically the last
PD3 of a type unique to Ribble, worked the 22.55 from Blackpool
to Morecambe, being greeted by a gathering including several
cowboys, who gave it a seven-gun salute. Things were more
sombre at Preston, where 1729 is seen arriving at the bus station
on the final day, a rainbow adding to the sense of history.
Joe Gornall

◄ Full OMO, whilst without doubt being the saviour of many a bus
route, was not received in all quarters with the same enthusiasm,
as is apparent from this work from the pen of a renowned, prolific
(and anonymous!) scribe deep within Ribble's Preston empire.
courtesy Liz and Philip Wilson

Chris Moyes, undertaking a three-week comparative course at Ribble in 1973 after his NBC training scheme, was impressed by the scale but appalled by the bureaucracy, discovering that it felt much bigger than other companies. Financial problems escalated: in 1975 the Company faced its biggest-ever cost increases, totalling £3¼ million, and fares rose again, to very high levels. Ribble took the decision to go down the path of Agency Agreements — a move influenced by the number of other operators in its area. In effect it became the operating arm of the new powerful councils, of which Lancashire County Council was probably one of the most dynamic. Ribble also entered agreements with Merseyside and Greater Manchester Passenger Transport Authorities. The NBC Market Analysis Project was carried out in a somewhat half-hearted way; Chris Moyes returned to co-ordinate this and wondered whether, as a result of these agreements, the Company had lost its ability to understand the market.

It fell to Ian Chapman, General Manager from 1979, to steer Ribble through the implications of the 1985 Transport Act, Deregulation and Privatisation. The tale of holding together the staff as the Company was chopped up into smaller bits, introduced minibuses and was involved in massive competition is for another place. So is the privatisation — a complex deal concluded on 2 March 1988 — the 63rd NBC sale. It is mentioned only because the successful team felt that the Ribble name was still strong enough for their new venture. Sadly subsequent owners don't feel the same way.

Where it counts, with people, the name is still very much alive and fondly remembered. Ribble buses may have gone, but the Ribble 'family' most certainly has not.

You can almost smell the woodsmoke as series B National 808 from 1979 leaves Chapel Stile in November 1986 on its way down Langdale. The headlights illuminate the dry-stone walls (which, as it's raining, are wet dry-stone walls), and in the background is one of the famous Pikes. This could only be the Lake District. It's also an unusual time, featuring a deregulated but still State-owned bus. *Roger Davies*

A taste of things to come. Ribble's first Tiger Cub coach, with Burlingham Seagull bodywork — 946, dating from 1954 — was sold to McLennan of Spitalfield in 1968. Here it is at the latter's premises in July 1971. The purchase of McLennan's was to be a significant early step in the growth of the Stagecoach empire . . . *Michael Dryhurst*

Given all that happened to it, the build-up to Deregulation in 1986 was particularly fraught for Ribble, and any thoughts of privatisation had to wait for the newly down-sized company to settle down. It was considered vital that staff be kept in the picture, and the management team arranged a series of hotpot suppers (with free prize draws) around the patch, to do just that. A radio jingle (somewhat tongue-in-cheek) was produced, and the annual sports presentations were made by Samantha Fox. Meanwhile, to ensure the Company was 'just the ticket', Linda Lusardi rallied the troops in a new staff newspaper, the *Ribble Rouser*, which also included a cartoon of the doubtful actions of the 'Blue Streak' bus company.

Mike Shires Ribble collection